Kids in the Biz

A Hollywood Handbook
for Parents

Troy A. Rutter

Foreword by Paul Petersen

HEINEMANN
Portsmouth, NH

Heinemann
A division of Reed Elsevier Inc.
361 Hanover Street
Portsmouth, NH 03801–3912
www.heinemanndrama.com

Offices and agents throughout the world

© 2005 by Troy A. Rutter

All rights reserved. No part of this book may be reproduced in any form or by any electronic or mechanical means, including information storage and retrieval systems, without permission in writing from the publisher, except by a reviewer, who may quote brief passages in a review.

Library of Congress Cataloging-in-Publication Data
Rutter, Troy A.
    Kids in the biz : a Hollywood handbook for parents / Troy A. Rutter.
        p. cm.
    ISBN 0-325-00708-X (alk. paper)
    1. Acting—Vocational guidance—United States.   2. Child actors—United States.   I. Title.

PN2055.R88 2004
792'.023'73—dc22   2004017182

Editor: Lisa A. Barnett
Production: Lynne Costa
Cover design: Cathy Hawkes, Cat & Mouse
Typesetter: TechBooks
Manufacturing: Steve Bernier

Printed in the United States of America on acid-free paper
09 08 07 06 05   VP   1 2 3 4 5

CONTENTS

CONTENTS

FOREWORD

"Just seeing a kid in show business tells you a lot about the parents" is a show business truism first written by Lonnie Burr, one of the original Mouseketeers. What was true in Lonnie's day remains the same today . . . with one critical difference: education.

Today's show business parents have access to a wide variety of information sources and how-to manuals that my mother, for example, would have gladly paid for back in the day. Following the formation of a former kid star "club" called A Minor Consideration in 1990 and a whole series of well-publicized tragedies and equally well-publicized legal advances in the world of working children, learning the nuts and bolts of successfully raising a child in the world of the performing arts suddenly got a whole lot easier.

From actually getting that first headshot to finding a qualified theatrical agent, the ways and means of handling "the business" are now in print and veterans of show business have begun to share their knowledge instead of treating the lessons they learned (and mistakes they made) as privately held business secrets.

I cannot stress highly enough the crucial role that education plays in the lives of both our talented children and our savvy stage parents. Education is a continuing process, from getting started to overseeing the dozens of financial opportunities a successful breakout performance can create, and it is a wise parent who seeks every possible means of educating himself about protecting his growing child.

There is more to show business than meets the eye, and the balancing act all parents must play means they have to thoughtfully weigh and carefully measure the often competing pressures of character development, age-appropriate behaviors, talent enhancement, scholastic performance, and money management.

Troy Rutter has laid out a road map for the parent who knows she must never stop the process of learning about the business her child finds so appealing. Common sense will tell you that in the rapidly changing world of developing children and expanding business opportunities, keeping yourself informed is the surest way to protect your child.

Always remember that "too much of a good thing" is reality when it comes to show business. A solid foundation and continuous self-examination help young actors and their parents avoid most of the pitfalls and traps of a very seductive undertaking. Pay attention and always have an exit strategy.

Good luck.

—Paul Petersen
President and Founder of A Minor Consideration
www.minorcon.org

ACKNOWLEDGMENTS

There are many people who have made a tremendous impact on the creation of this book and to whom I wish to express my sincerest gratitude. First to my mom, who let me move not only out of the house but out of the state and to Hollywood. Thank you to my friends and family, who also supported me and kept my mom from going crazy whenever I called home about my adventures. To the many industry folks who contributed to my knowledge: Bob Jamieson of Noble Media Group, Paul Petersen, Tim and Sally Gamble, Dino May, Rob Wuertz, Jim Moloshok, and the many managers, agents, and others who all made a difference.

Thank you also to the many young actors and actresses who allowed me to watch them at work and at play: Mason Gamble, Kevin Zegers, Elijah Wood, Ryan Merriman, Eric Lloyd, Wil Horneff, Scott Terra, Debi and Dylan Patton, David Gallagher, Dylan and Casey Boersma, Marylou and Emilee Greenberg, Scott and Melanie Cox, and the countless others I have met and learned from.

A very special thanks to my editor, Lisa Barnett, and the staff at Heinemann for seeing something special in this book and providing invaluable advice and guidance.

And to the many actors of all ages I have been privileged to know. Thanks to you all.

INTRODUCTION

If you are reading this, chances are either you are already located in one of the performing arts capitals, or you are getting ready to pack up the car and head out to the Wild Wild West. In the first case, great! You are in one of the best places to begin your child's career. In the case of the latter, however . . . hold on! Don't go dreaming of strawberry smoothies just yet.

There are opportunities for young performers starting out in the business everywhere you look, even in your own backyard. I'm from Iowa, a place that you would not expect to be the cornerstone of *any kind* of Hollywood production.

Wrong.

While in Iowa, I saw an enormous amount of opportunities as a young aspiring actor. There were local casting calls for *The Bridges of Madison Country, Field of Dreams, Twister,* and the TV movie of the week with our very own Tom Arnold, *The Woman Who Loved Elvis.* Quite a bit of work for the middle of nowhere! When you talk about Iowan actors, who can forget Elijah Wood, John Wayne, and Ashton Kutcher?

But it does not stop there. Television is also a huge market in small communities. *Rescue 911* frequented my area. Additionally, there are several local commercials to be found. I remember working through college at the local ABC affiliate and just by chance asking if they needed a different voice for some commercials. They jumped at the opportunity to provide yet one more voice for clients!

On an even smaller scale, there is cable public access television. What could be better than showing off your child's talent on public access? Some programs are even syndicated around the country, giving even more exposure.

Aside from television and movies, there are also local theatre opportunities. From high school to college to community theatre to the Guthrie Theater in Minneapolis—opportunities abound to practice your craft *everywhere*. Plus there are movies and television shows shot on location everywhere around the country.

As I mentioned, there is one key thing to remember when starting to seek a career for your child in the entertainment field, or "the industry," or simply "the biz": Acting is not just television and movies. Sure, it may be more rewarding to see your child's name on a movie poster in thousands of theatres around the world, or see his name come across the television during the movie of the week, but the craft of acting is what it is all about.

So keep an open mind and your head from the clouds. It is a lot of work. But if you and your child are willing to make it work, the rewards are out there for the taking.

In the immortal words of Walt Disney—

THINK, BELIEVE, DREAM, DARE!

CHAPTER

1

What It Takes

RECENTLY I WAS ASKED BY A FAMILY FRIEND HOW TO GET her son into television and films—the biz. I asked her why she thought that her eight-year-old wanted to pursue this particular career instead of something that boys traditionally dream about being when they grow up, like a police officer or fireman. She rattled off a list of reasons that included "he wants to star with John Travolta," "he wants to make a lot of money," and "he wants to live near the beach." When I talked with her son he told me simply, "I'm tired of shoveling snow!"

As a parent, you are inundated with sometimes extreme requests from your child. But what do you do when your son or daughter tells you, "I want to be an actor."? Many parents dismiss it right away, telling their child, "That's nice, dear, now go play." The fact is that every young performer in the business had to start someplace. There are a few simple traits that can indicate whether or not your child will have a successful and long career in the TV or movie business. If your child is

- energetic,
- outspoken,
- excited about meeting new people,
- good in school,
- eager to try new things, and
- creative,

then congratulations, you may have a star just waiting to be discovered. Talk with your child and make sure she understands this is going to take commitment from the entire family to work on this goal and it is not something that is going to happen next week, next month, or maybe even next year.

As with every major decision, there are good and bad reasons for wanting to get into the entertainment business. Many children have an unrealistic view of the salaries they can expect to take home. (This will be covered in Chapter 14, "Money.") Sometimes parents may want to have their child in the business so that they can manage their child and not work a "real" job. These are very poor reasons for getting your child started in such an emotionally and physically demanding business, yet I have heard both of them and others described in countless horror stories from agents and managers. The important piece of the puzzle is your child. Think about your child's welfare and whether this will make him a happy, complete person or if you are doing it for your own benefit. If you think about the long term—say, ten to fifteen years down the road, or until your child turns eighteen—you will usually make the right decision.

Many parents simply do not think their child could make it in the entertainment business, so in order to save their child from embarrassment, they redirect the child's energy into a sport or dance. Kids tune into this right away and will see through it. The truth is there is not one look that will guarantee your child will be the next Tom Cruise or Elijah Wood. Young performers can be successful no matter how they look: short, tall, fat, skinny, freckles, birthmarks, you name it. I know a young performer whose eyes are two different colors—one is brown and the other blue! The point is that no matter what your child looks like, if she wants it badly enough and if she is encouraged enough, she'll find the work.

Looks aside, most casting directors when looking to fill a role will look for the youngster who wins them over with her talent and charm. This is especially true at the local level, where the casting notice might simply be "girl age 8–14." As you get further and further with your child's career, the level of detail contained in the casting notices will be greater and greater. Enjoy the open calls now and have fun with your child.

SIBLING RIVALRY

It is common to have more than one child in the family express their interest in performing when another one does after they see the attention and support their sibling is getting. In fact, for many parents, especially single parents, it is easier and more convenient to have more than one child going on auditions. Regardless of whether or not your other children are interested in performing, there will undoubtedly be some conflict between the children and between the children and the adults. Perhaps one child feels that you are spending more time with the sibling, or maybe they both audition for the same part. You will find that dealing with the rivalry can sometimes be a job in and of itself.

Already in this chapter you have heard about the importance of making the child's career a family decision and everybody having his or her own role. This will be also be echoed in later chapters, but it fits in well here when talking about the role of the siblings in a family with a child performer. At your family meetings, keep the lines of communication open with your other children so they have a part in the decision making. By doing so, you will help ease the ego of the other children and make them feel like they are contributing something as well. This is also a good time to have the family talk together about what is going on with all the children—grades, sports, and so on. Over the past few years we have heard about families spending less and less time together, but those families who have their special meetings continue to be happier and healthier families—get into the habit!

Parents need to be careful when dolling out praise for their young performer, especially in the presence of the other children. All children need to be praised for what they have done correctly or accomplished, but praising your young actor for every little thing may cause resentment among the other children and their friends. Likewise, allowing your child to have tantrums either on the set or at an audition or to talk back to you will get him in trouble later on and should not be tolerated. As a child progresses in his career, it is important that both praise and punishment are dealt with seriously and kept in balance. A child who is earning good money by performing may soon start thinking that he is the major breadwinner in the family and start making irrational demands of family members about where money should be put. By keeping your child's head on straight from the beginning, you can help avoid the Hollywood brat syndrome early and provide a better environment for all concerned.

COMMITMENT

Before starting your child down the road of becoming a paid performer, you should sit down with her and have a talk about commitment. This is best done as a family meeting scenario and you should include everybody in the discussion. Being a performer requires more than just ambition; it requires a level of commitment that your child should be mature enough to understand and accept.

How many times has your child left his homework undone until the night before it was due? How many times have you had to do your child's paper route when she did not get up on time or refused to get up at all? Becoming a serious actor or actress is a much larger commitment than doing a chore or job once a week. Your child should be acutely aware of the type of commitment he or she is making. From training, to performances, to hygiene—it will require a tremendous amount of energy to persevere and succeed as a performer.

Commitment means more than just going to an acting class once a week. The true meaning and trial of the word *commitment* often comes when something better than what your child is currently doing is offered. For instance, suppose your child gets a national commercial offer and the production company wants to fly you to Chicago on the same weekend that a local play your child is in is having its opening performance? It would be unfair to the theatre production if you up and left on a whim, hoping that another child in the play could step up into your child's vacant role.

A definite conflict arises when talking about commitment with your child. On one hand, you need to provide encouragement and let your child know that it is OK if he wants to go back to being a normal kid. On the other hand, starting a career as a performer does take a dedication of at least one to two years of your child's life to even begin to show any results. Because of this, I recommend that the commitment you talk about with your child be limited to only a period of, say, two years to begin with. If after two years your child decides he wants to do something else, let him do it. Two years may sound like a long time to your child, and possibly to you as well, but families expecting to achieve an overnight sensation are most often very disappointed.

UPS AND DOWNS

It goes without saying that parents need to be supportive of their kids. I firmly believe every parent who starts down the path of helping her or his child become a performer starts out with good intentions. However, there are changes that occur over time in which the parent comes to resemble the stereotypical stage mom that instills fear in kids, family members, and relatives alike. To be fair, there are also a number of stage dads that are equally misguided in how they handle their child's career. However, for some reason, the press is much more lenient on fathers.

There are always slow times in a child's career, whether it is in your community or in the big cities of New York and Los Angeles. Dealing with the slow times is an art itself. It requires a good deal of patience and understanding from you, the parent, to help your child maintain her sense of self-esteem and worth. There are times when you will wonder if it is worth it, and kids are quick to pick up on this. Dealing with the slow times is difficult, but the old saying is true that show business is 90 percent show and 10 percent business.

Having a slow period can help your child concentrate on his or her current schoolwork or try something new. Perhaps she has not been attending her Scout meetings as regularly as she might have wanted and is just inches away from a new badge. Maybe he never had time to test for his green belt in tae kwon do. Slow periods for young performers offer a great chance for a kid to just be a kid. Hanging out with friends, laughing, going to a movie, studying—all of these things should not be underrated when it comes to your child. Take time to let your child have fun and she will continue to find performing fun as well.

Another way to beat the slow times is to more aggressively involve your child in the day-to-day business of acting. You can have him contact the local theatre company to find out when the next auditions are, or you can have him search on the Internet for the name and address of a particular commercial production company or agency. The more you involve your child from the beginning, the more he will understand the hard work you are doing for him—and should your child ever go professional, maybe he will not be so quick to question the 15 percent you charge for being his manager!

GETTING OUT

At first glance, it may seem a bit odd to be including this subject in the first chapter of this book. After some consideration, however, I realized how important it was to present this subject early on, rather than wait until after the other chapters on local and national work. It is an important issue that presents itself every so often during a child's career as interest wanes in the face of rejection and slow periods of work. Indeed, it is a bit of a contradiction with the material earlier in this chapter on commitment, but the bottom line is that when your child honestly comes to you and says he has had enough, it is over.

How you react to your child's decision to get out of the business is a key factor in determining whether your child is serious or if she is just gauging whether or not you want her to quit. Those who stomp their feet and preach to their children about all the hard work and how much money they have put into their child's career will find that even though their child's mind is really made up, he might continue to go through the motions rather than risk having his parents be mad at him. This will lead to a bad performance and an equally bad attitude on the set, making the entire cast and crew miserable.

If your child approaches you and wants to give up acting, the best thing to do is simply listen. You will be able to tell right away if your child really wants to stop or if there are other things going on. Maybe her classmates are making fun of her or maybe she really wanted that last commercial and is devastated she did not get it. Whatever the case may be, listening and not interrupting will help bring out your child's real desires and feelings.

If your child is in the middle of a play or has given a commitment to another production or job, you should talk to him about honoring the choices he has made and let him know he can stop after he has fulfilled all of his current obligations. It is far easier to stop performing when your child is still at the local level than if you have already relocated to a bigger city in search of work. It is because of this that I suggest making a deal with your child from the beginning. When I worked with a singing group of four brothers, The Moffatts, I witnessed one of the best examples of commitment, choices, and empowerment that I have ever seen. Their father, Frank Moffatt, told me that he made a deal with each of the four brothers to commit to five years of rehearsing, record-ing, touring, and performing. Each of the guys gave his word and although it was not a formal contract, each of them adhered to that promise. When the five years were up, the decision came up again. This time, the brothers decided as a group that some of their tastes in music were changing and it was best to separate and dissolve the group.

It is not too much to ask your young child for this type of unwritten contract. Any book and any person will tell you that getting started as a professional performer will take time. One year is perhaps wishful thinking. In reality, it could take two or more years before the career is profitable. Some parents will even make up a typed contract that they will have their kid sign so they can remind their child of the commit-ment she made when she wants to quit. While this is extreme, it is not an altogether bad idea—it teaches the importance of making choices and reaffirms that the entire family is involved in that child's decision to pursue acting.

2

CHAPTER

Starting Local

ONE OF THE MYTHS PERPETUATED THROUGH THE POPULAR media over the years has been that to make it in commercials and films, you have to pack up and move to Los Angeles or New York to get your career on track. However, there are many opportunities for young performers in and around your hometown, and the competition is actually much less stiff. You just need to know how to find them and how to get them.

Having your child's first experience with building his career in his hometown allows him to be comfortable in an environment that he knows and feels safe in. Gaining experience in your own community will also allow your child to build up his credentials and résumé so he will have something to show when the day comes that your child wants to go for the big time. Having the support of you, his friends, and other family members and familiar people is very important in this critical stage when your child is forming who he is and what his goals are.

COMMUNITY AND SCHOOL THEATRE

A great opportunity for young performers is participating in the local theatre program. Many cities have community theatres or college theatres that perform several productions per year or season. Call or write to request their current newsletter and their schedule of events for the season. Keep on top of the audition material. If you know they are planning to put on a production of *Oliver!* in a few months, rent the film and start practicing; it will give your child an advantage even if they do not have your child sing one of the songs for the audition.

Auditions for local productions seldom require any professional tools such as photos and résumés, so when you arrive at the audition usually there will be a sign-in form that will ask for your child's name, age, and what part she is auditioning for. Your child may be asked to perform a short monologue or sing a common song such as "America the Beautiful" in the key of C. Your coaching at this level, and every level, should be supportive. Make sure she knows to fully announce herself when she walks onto the stage and to speak up. When she is done with the audition, tell her she has done a great job and then do something fun! The following couple of days can be stressful for your child, so do not add to her frustration level. Let her know she did her best, and if it happens, it happens. If your child sees your anxiety level up, it will magnify itself a hundred times in her.

Another avenue your child may explore is a larger role in a bigger city's theatre. The same rules apply; however, you should remind your child that this and all performing work is a commitment. It would be very unprofessional to simply quit a production if your child is cast for a guest spot on a national television show. If your child wants to do theatre, it will usually consume a good two to three months of his time in rehearsals and performances, so make sure that expectations are clearly laid out before he begins auditioning.

School plays and musicals should not be regarded as being too amateur for the aspiring performer. In fact, because these performances are with your child's peers, they provide great experience in a familiar environment. The frequency of school plays varies depending on the grade level of your child. Most elementary schools may put on four chorus events a year and perhaps a once-a-year play for the parents. Secondary schools sometimes have twice the amount of chorus performances as well as fall, winter, and spring plays with a musical or student-directed one-acts as well.

In elementary school productions, there is generally not an organized audition process; in fact, in the case of classroom productions, every child in the class may be expected to participate. Younger children will enjoy being a rock or a tree or wildlife critters, while children in fourth to sixth grade tend to be more interested in traditional speaking roles. Because these early plays and performances include everyone in the class, there is little or no direct competition and the main emphasis is on having fun. If your child is in the fifth or sixth grade and enjoys putting on puppet shows, maybe he would like to do a show for the kindergarteners and first graders in the school.

Junior and senior high school productions begin to take the form of traditional auditions in which the students compete for the leading roles in the play or musical. In junior or middle school musicals, while there are the leads in the production, every student who auditions will usually end up in a chorus if she is not selected for one of the main roles. While it may not be the most glamorous or exciting role in the production, the chorus is an integral part of these productions and the chorus members may actually be on stage more than the lead characters!

At the high school level, things are even more competitive for the leading roles and while not every student will make it into the production, there are positions for everybody in the scenery, prop, and costume departments. Oftentimes the director of the production has a feeling for whom he wants to cast in a particular play before the auditions begin based on his previous experience with the juniors and seniors of the school. Auditions will consist of a reading selection from the play's script and perhaps a song of the student's choosing if it is a musical. The director will post a list of the students and the roles outside his office or classroom and eager young actors will wait impatiently to see if their name is on the list. If your child does not get the part she wanted, encourage her to participate in the production on one of the other crews.

Many high schools also have a student organization called Thespians, which is short for a troupe sanctioned by the International Thespian Society and organized by the Educational Theatre Association. Members are inducted into the Thespian Society by their peers and also by accumulating points by participating in high school productions and managing students in set construction, costumes, makeup, directing, and other areas of interest. Once inducted into the group, students must maintain a high degree of involvement in the school's drama program to remain active members. If your child is involved in the drama productions, he will probably know if his school has a Thespian troupe. If the school does not have one, contact the drama or English department chair to see if she would help organize one at your child's school.

LOCAL COMMERCIALS

Another great opportunity for young performers in their hometowns are the local network affiliates such as NBC, CBS, ABC, and even Fox and WB. These stations, as well as your local cable company, produce the majority of commercials for local businesses throughout their viewing area. Listen carefully and you will probably hear the same voice over and over again on a variety of different local commercials.

At each television station there are individuals who are in charge of making these commercials. Most stations will refer to this job as creative services. A great way to start getting work is to simply write these stations and let them know that your child is available in case an opportunity comes up in which they need a kid swooshing down the water slide or running around a baseball diamond. In your letter, be sure to let them know that you are a local resident and also what your child's availability is. You can include a short résumé of theatre credits and also an instant snapshot or standard 4-by-6-inch close-up photo of your child's face. Thank them for their consideration and include your phone number. Here's an example of such a letter:

> Dear [name of creative services manager],
>
> I am writing to you in regard to any opportunities you may have for my [son/daughter] in any upcoming local commercials you are working on for your clients. Enclosed is a photograph for your reference. We can be contacted at 555-1212 and we look forward to hearing from you.
>
> Regards,
>
> [name of parent]

It is important that you get in the habit of obtaining the specific name of the person you are writing to instead of referring to him simply as commercial producer or creative services manager. This practice will carry on to the later stages of your child's career when approaching the agencies and casting directories directly.

There are opportunities like this in every community, but you may have to travel to the nearest big city to find the most work. As your child performs in a play or does a voice-over for the local swimming pool, she'll gain not only experience for her résumé but also confidence in her talents and abilities. This local work also allows you to judge if your child has the ambition and dedication to take it to the next level.

Once your child has a few theatre roles and maybe a couple of commercials under his belt, you may feel pressure from relatives and friends to go professional. They might ask to see your son's headshot or his demo reel, leaving you making excuses about why you do not have one. Do not let anybody pressure you or your child into steps you are not prepared for. At this stage in your child's career, those extra promotional tools really are not needed; your 4-by-6 color photo will be more than enough to suffice until you decide to branch out into the larger markets.

The Demo Tape

A voice-over is a short commercial that features one or more voices trying to sell a product or service. The availability of voice-over work exists in every size market from the small town to national spots. To go after these commercials, it is a good idea to put together a simple recording of your child reading different types of commercials. This recording is referred to as a *demo tape* and can be duplicated and sent to local television and radio stations as well as used to obtain an agent that specializes in voice-over work.

Since most voice-overs do not have your child physically on camera, you should encourage your child to be creative in how he portrays the different characters he plays. This can be a fun way to do work if you plan it out right. The best way to get practice doing voice-overs is to record several commercials from television or the radio and write out a script from each for your child to practice with. It does not matter if the commercial has a male, female, older, or younger voice in the real commercial—that is where part of the fun is! Record your child doing the commercials and play them back for him. He will quickly realize if he has a problem pronouncing certain words and will probably ask to do them again and again. Work on these commercials and have your child try emphasizing different words each time through. Another fun exercise is to have your child read the same commercial but pretend to be old, from the South, or from England or try other different accents and personalities.

Once in a while you can slip in a brand-new commercial you secretly prepared when your child wasn't looking to see how she reacts to new copy. Have your child read through the script once quickly, and then ask her what she thinks the person in the script is feeling. Remember, at this stage there really are no right and wrong answers; the point of this exercise is to have your child make a choice. Next, have your child read the script with the same energy and determination she has been using on the material she is familiar with. Being presented with new material on the spot is known as *cold reading*. The quicker your child can read and understand a script, the better chance she has of being confident in her own performance and thus the better chance she has of getting a callback on a real audition. Cold reading strikes fear into the minds and hearts of even seasoned actors, but with patience and practice it can become just as natural to your child as performing something she already knows.

With just these few steps you are introducing your child to a learning experience right away. You have taught him to make a determined choice when reading new material, and by listening to his own performances and critiquing them, you are also providing guidance for the material and for your child's mental well-being. It is much easier for kids to accept the suggestions of others when they are expecting guidance and suggestions than if they are told everything they do is perfect.

If you find material both you and your child like that you feel showcases her best work, record the commercial on a brand-new cassette tape. If available, you may also choose to buy a five-minute cassette tape at your local music or audio store. With compact disc recorders being sold with nearly every new computer these days, some innovative parents have hooked up a microphone to their computers so they can digitize and edit commercials on the computer.

The average length for a demo tape is only two to three minutes at the most, so the idea is to keep it simple, short, and sweet. When a casting director or agent listens to your child's tape, he will allow only ten to fifteen seconds to decide if your child is right for the part or for his agency. Their first demo tape should include two to three short commercials and be clearly labeled with your child's name and your agent's phone number if you have one. If your child does not yet have an agent, your home phone number or message service will do. In the early stages of your child's career, it is not necessary to hire an outside production company to record, edit, and produce your child's demo tape. Doing so at this point in her career would be a waste of time and money, so keep it simple. You can find labels and sleeves for audiocassettes and compact discs at your local office supply store. These are usually white and contain guides to help you align them in your printer so they look professional.

It is possible to do all the cassette duplication yourself at this early stage. A regular boom box with one player and one cassette recorder will suffice. Avoid using the high-speed dub feature as this tends to make the voice a slightly higher pitch than normal. You are not going for an excessive number of copies at the beginning, so a pack of eight or ten tapes will be sufficient for your first mailings.

Looking for voice-over work in your local area can be done in conjunction with mailing out your child's headshot and résumé. The first places to send your package to would be the local television stations, followed by the local radio stations. A simple, to-the-point cover letter is enough to introduce your child and provide contact information in case the station has any need for your child's talents in the future. When you mail out a cassette tape or a compact disc, you should take care to provide adequate packaging so the media is not broken or scratched in the process.

LOCAL TRAINING

There is good news and bad news about local training opportunities for young performers outside of Los Angeles. The bad news: there are few, if any, programs targeted directly to advancing your child's career in the entertainment industry. The good news: every experience is a learning opportunity.

Modeling and/or acting classes are available in many big cities; check the one nearest your hometown for these training opportunities. Most will allow you to audit their classes for one or two sessions. These sessions may include introductory courses, on-camera acting, modeling, runway techniques, commercials, and makeup techniques. The problem with many of these workshops is that they will oftentimes charge an exorbitant amount of money to get into the classes and then will ask you to go to their preferred photographer, who will charge several hundred dollars for photographs your child is not even ready for yet.

There are legitimate classes and workshops out there; you just have to be careful when selecting the right one for your child. There is a large national company that preys on aspiring performers and their parents by setting up booths in local malls and encouraging kids to try out and sign on with their national agency. Unfortunately, this company tends to change its name about every six months, so it is impossible to give you a definite name to look out for. You can protect your child (and your pocketbook) by thoroughly researching any company offering classes and talking to parents that have children in the program and getting their opinion on how the classes are helping their children.

Every experience your child has in pursuing his performing career will have an educational effect on his career. Each audition he attends will strengthen his skills and confidence. Every time he sings "America the Beautiful" will be better than the time before. You have probably heard celebrities speak during interviews about paying their dues in the early stages of their careers. Your child will attend countless auditions for every real piece of work he is hired to do. Indeed, not only is the audition itself a learning experience, but your child will learn rather quickly that he will not be able to book every job he auditions for. This is why it is extremely important to be supportive of your child as well as let him know the reality of the process and amount of rejection he will receive.

WHEN HOLLYWOOD COMES TO TOWN

There are times when a film or a television series will choose to go on location for a particular scene or series of scenes in a production. There are just some locations that cannot be re-created inside a soundstage or in southern California. For these shoots, the production company will hire a location scout who will find the best remote location for filming. These location shoots provide a tremendous opportunity for the local performer who wants to build her résumé with more professional experience.

Nearly every state has a film office that is run by a state entity such as economic affairs or the tourism office. When location scouts are searching for the perfect place, often they approach the film offices in a particular region first to have an initial idea of what will work well for the project. The film office is generally staffed by only a few individuals; however, it offers a wealth of information on past, present, and possible future productions in your state.

You can find out what major television and feature films are in the state by writing the office and requesting information on what is filming where. To help in your search, I have included a list of all the state film offices in Appendix 3. You may also want to ask if the film office has a production handbook for the state. This handbook features professional craftspeople, camera operators, lighting designers, contractors, and other categories of professionals who are available if a production comes into the area. Most state film handbooks also have a section for talent, although this section may be confined to only talent agencies. In your letter, you can ask to have your child included in the talent section of the handbook or ask if you can receive the handbook.

An example letter that includes all of these suggestions follows:

Dear [name of director of film office],

My name is [name] and my [son/daughter] is an aspiring [actor/actress] who is currently building a résumé by doing community productions and commercials. I understand that many feature films and television series sometimes shoot on location and would appreciate it if you would send me a current listing of any such filming being done in the state now or in the near future. In addition, please send me information on how to include my child in your state production handbook as well as how to obtain a copy of the handbook for our personal use.

Thank you for your time and assistance in these matters. I look forward to hearing from you.

There are other ways you can hear about big-time productions in your area as well. The local news will often run a feature story when a production comes to town. A professional publication, *The Hollywood*

Reporter, also lists films in development and where they will be filming. The *Reporter* is a daily publication so the cost for a regular subscription is rather high; however, it also offers production listings as part of the content on its website at *www.hollywoodreporter.com* for a modest fee of $19.95 per month.

When a production comes to town casting directors will let the local media know if and when they will be conducting auditions for local performers and people who are interested in being part of the film. Usually these calls are only for background performers, or extras, who will not have a speaking part. When a production conducts local casting, they will have a designated day or two on the weekend that they will be registering people to appear in the film.

My first experience with a location casting call was on the film *Twister*, directed by Jan de Bont. The production company set up two small trailers near the motel they were staying at in town and set a call time for Saturday and Sunday at 8 A.M. Thinking I would get there early, I arrived at 6 A.M. and was greeted by a line the size of which I had not seen since I went to see *Star Wars* when I was a kid. The lesson here is that these location casting calls will usually take all day because of the sheer number of people who want a piece of the Hollywood magic. If a call is for 8 A.M., there will be people there at 4 A.M. and definitely 5 A.M. Plan accordingly for the weather and the long wait times. Bring along some inexpensive cloth folding chairs to make the long wait somewhat comfortable.

Once the line starts to move, the excitement and energy around you and your child will build and build until it is your child's turn to go into the trailer or the main room. When it is your child's turn, you will be given a slip of paper that will have blanks for all of the usual information such as name, contact information, age, height, weight, and so on. It will also have a special section for wardrobe requirements, such as waist size, inseam, shirt size, shoe size, and so on, so it would be a good idea to accumulate this information beforehand. There will also be a spot near the bottom of the page where they will attach an instant photograph of your child that they will take when you reach that point in line. This may also be completely computerized using a digital camera.

The entire process is streamlined and efficient. Once you get into the main building, they will rush you through in a matter of minutes so that when you are done you'll be left with a feeling of "That's it?" Congratulations! You have suddenly realized the secret mantra of show business: hurry up and wait!

REALITY TELEVISION

With the continued popularity of so-called reality shows on networks of all sizes, the sad truth is that scripted shows have indeed suffered a decline since the 2000 premiere of *Survivor*. Taking one look over the primetime schedules shows that these reality television shows dominate the time slots in which the most popular scripted shows were once shown. While this is definitely disheartening and has contributed to an increase in unemployment rates for actors and actresses, the good news is there is an increasing number of independent films and short-lived television projects. Hopefully the future will show a revived interest in genuine, scripted programs.

There are ways for children to participate in reality programs but they are extremely limited. Reality television for kids consists of a mixture of game shows and spin-offs of adult television shows. Game shows for kids were first introduced on the Nickelodeon network and included shows such as *Double Dare*, *Masters of the Maze*, *Fun House*, and a list of others that seemed to all be messy and require somebody with a squeegee offstage. Those looking to go the reality television route should pay close attention to these types of shows, which air on Saturday mornings on the major networks. ABC has Disney programming, CBS has Nickelodeon, and NBC is partnered with the Discovery Channel.

One of the most popular shows at the time of writing was a takeoff of TLC's *Trading Spaces*. In *Trading Spaces; Boys vs. Girls,* two boys and two girls redecorate each other's rooms with the help of a carpenter and an interior designer. Application forms for the show can be found on the Discovery Channel website at *www.discovery.com*. The process by which applicants are selected is clearly laid out regardless of the program your child is applying to be on. Like *Trading Spaces*, most reality television shows put their applications on their website. This helps the program not only collect the applications and go through them but also clearly state the rules for the program, such as where you live, your age, and so on.

The *Survivor* craze has also given way to a similar game show also shown on NBC on Saturday mornings called *Endurance*. Instead of tribes, kids are grouped into different-colored teams and perform a variety of intellectual and physical challenges to collect pieces of a pyramid that symbolize strength, heart, courage, perseverance, luck, trust, leadership, discipline, knowledge, commitment, teamwork, and ingenuity. The team who collects all twelve pieces first wins the game.

Not all reality shows revolve around physical challenges and teamwork. The popularity of *American Idol* has created a whole new onslaught of talent search competitions. These include traditional talent competitions such as singing and dancing as well as novelty acts and special talents. Young performer Scott Cox appeared with his singing group Gimme 5 on the Ed McMahon show *Next Big Star* before launching his solo career (see Chapter 4 to learn more about Scott). Mario Lopez, of *Saved by the Bell* fame, is now hosting many different competition-type shows, including *America's Most Talented Kid*. In addition, *Star Search* has been known to do a show for kids, and children are also seen on a show called *Performing As*, in which performers dress up and perform as their idols.

There is a debate among the performing community as to what constitutes a professional performer. Shows such as *Star Search* are listed as amateur competitions. There have been cases, however, in which lesser-known celebrities have competed under the amateur title on these shows. For instance, there was a young performer who appeared on the *Jenny Jones Show* and entered the Internet contest for Ed McMahon's *Next Big Star* before he competed and was a semifinalist on *Star Search*. Opinions vary as to whether or not this is ethical and fair to the other competitors. Melanie Cox, mother of Scott Cox, is adamantly opposed to young actors and semiprofessional performers appearing on amateur shows. While her son, Scott, got his big break on Ed McMahon's *Next Big Star*, because he has appeared with two musical groups since then and has a television career, she will not allow him to enter these talent competitions anymore.

Steve Harvey hosts a popular television show called *Steve Harvey's Big Time* where novelty acts perform and do crazy things. Some of the types of acts that Harvey has shown include a scientist who creates flammable bubbles as well as a competition between a man and a boy to see who could hold the most grits on his clothes after spinning around in a grit-filled metal basin. Harvey's quick wit and delivery make this show popular with all age groups. Similarly, David Letterman often has children on his show for the "Stupid Human Tricks" segment.

For some of these shows, as well as traditional game shows, there may be a requirement to live in a certain area. For instance, *Trading Spaces: Boys vs. Girls* asks applicants to list the closest metropolitan city. Most game shows for both kids and adults will conduct an initial interview first and then ask you to come back on a selected day to be a part of the contestant pool. Because of the extended time between interviews and the taping of the show, most contestants will have to live within an hour or two of the taping location. Read the requirements for contestants very carefully and if you have any questions, be sure to try to contact the show's staff and get answers.

3
CHAPTER

The Tools

YOU MAY HAVE ALREADY HEARD OTHER PARENTS OR actors around you refer to "the tools of the trade." You may also have been sitting next to someone at a local audition and had that parent pull out a crisp eight-by-ten-inch glossy headshot and ask to see yours, only to have the embarrassment of pulling out your four-by-six snapshot and muttering something along the lines of "the others are being reprinted." First off, if your child is working on a local level, there is absolutely no reason to be embarrassed about not having professional photos. There are exceptions of course, such as if your local area just happens to be a major entertainment center such as Los Angeles, New York, or even Chicago. But until you and your child decide to try the big time, stick with your color snapshots and laugh to yourself about how it would have been foolish to spend hundreds of dollars on photographs and duplicates that you do not need just yet.

There are many horror stories about parents dishing out hundreds of dollars for photographs that do not even look like their child—so do not do it! Children under the age of eighteen change so quickly, it would cost a fortune to have new photographs and reprints done every six months to a year. If you are in the local market, continue with the method that has been getting your child work. Keep it simple.

If, however, you are thinking about moving to the Los Angeles area, the playing field suddenly becomes more complex. *Everybody* in the town has a headshot he will be glad to show you at every opportunity. It is imperative upon arriving in L.A. that your child has the tools necessary to successfully market herself in the entertainment capital of the world. At a minimum, these tools include the photograph, the résumé, and the demo tape.

THE PHOTOGRAPH

The photograph is the first thing a potential casting director, agent, or manager will look at when determining if a child will fit into his production, agency, or management company. As such, it is important that your child's photograph yells, "Hire me! Hire me!" from the glossy paper on which it is printed. Getting the right photograph may seem difficult, but you can save yourself a lot of grief and frustration by remembering some very simple pointers.

First and foremost, the photograph has to actually look like your child. This may sound obvious, but I have seen several photos over the years that looked nothing at all like the children they were supposed to represent. Avoid airbrushing out freckles or moles and retouching the photo in any way. If your child has freckles, show them off! There is nothing worse than showing up at an audition and having the casting director ask, "Where's *this* girl?" while holding up a photo of your daughter that looks nothing like the young lady currently standing nervously in front of a group of strange people.

Choosing the right photographer is the key element in getting good photographs done. There are hundreds of potential photographers in the L.A. area who charge often outrageous fees for standard photographs. Before you choose one, do some research. You can find several books at the Samuel French bookstore on Ventura Boulevard on choosing the right photographer. Another good resource is the *Academy Players Directory*, which you can browse through at the Screen Actors Guild office. The *Players Directory* is a huge five-volume set of headshots as well as actors' representatives. Look through the children's section (usually Volume 5) and jot down the names of a few photographs that you like and their agents. In the back of the directory you will find addresses and phone numbers of all the talent agents and managers that are listed. You can try calling them up and politely asking if they know who took so-and-so's photograph. If they don't know, ask if they have a photographer they would recommend.

Once you have a list of potential photographers, call around and ask them if they have time to meet with you and your child so you can see some examples of their work. It is important that your child accompany you on this outing so she can get her own vibe from the photographer and you can gauge how comfortable your child is with him. The photographer's portfolio should obviously include other children and he should have a flyer or something you can take with you to look at later.

You should also ask a potential photographer her price for a standard sitting. Many photographers will try to get you to do multiple clothing changes and maybe even an on-location shoot. Stick to your guns and be firm that you will consider one to two changes for the headshots, but you are not looking for a modeling portfolio as of yet—just a simple headshot. Pricing for headshot photo sessions varies but will typically break down to about two or three rolls of film for $150 to $200. This will also include contact sheets, little thumbnails of every photo taken, and one or two eight-by-ten enlargements of photos of your choice. Additional enlargements are expensive—generally $10 to $20 each if you order them through the photographer. If the photographer offers a price outside this framework, simply thank her for her time and take her business card and sample and continue your search. The photographer may also tell you she can get you glossies for $5 each in mass quantities. Politely tell her you already work with a duplication house in town, but thank her for the offer.

After you have exhausted your list of potential photographers, sit down with your child and go over the samples and ask him which photographer he liked. If he did not like someone, move that person's material into another pile and continue going through the list. Once you have narrowed it down to two or three, try to remember the *Players Directory* photos you looked through. Could you see any of photographer A's photos being in there? How about photographer B's? If you cannot narrow it down and everybody seems about the same, then just pick one and make an appointment. Your child is growing and chances are he will need new photographs in a year—or less—so there will be plenty of other opportunities to try a new photographer in the months and years to come.

There are many different types of photographs that are used in the industry, but the only one you should worry about for the time being is the standard portrait, commonly referred to as a *headshot*. This type of photo is typically taken indoors in the photographer's studio rather than outside. A headshot is a photograph that should tell the casting director or agent what your child looks like now, so it is important that it accurately reflect your child's looks. The expressions in a headshot can range from a caricature to a more serious theatrical look. For now, it is best to stick with a simple headshot of your child smiling and looking happy and full of energy.

Expect and request that the photographer shoot different levels of smiling, serious, mischievous, and fun shots. This will help you later on when you choose certain photos for your mailings and others for a composite, a portfolio, and so on. You should always remain in the same room as your child when the shoot is going on. Never leave your child alone to answer a phone call or put more money in the parking meter. The moment you are gone, your child will lose some of the confidence and comfort level in what she is doing, so stay with her at all times.

Be sure to bring at least three to four changes of clothing and props if necessary with you to the photo shoot. There are a few things that you should be aware of to make the most out of the time with your photographer. First, do not get your child a haircut the night before or the day of your photo shoot. Try to wait at least a week after getting it cut before you have the photos done. This will give your child's hair a chance to find its new place and help it to stay in place. Keep a pair of sharp scissors with you just in case a curl creeps up behind the ear and just will not stay down. Also, spiked hair is out. If that is your child's normal haircut, you might want to convince him that it is time for a change. It is a lot easier to make it spiked down the road if the script calls for it.

Also, avoid heavy makeup. It is OK to bring some touch-up for your son or daughter just in case, but the photographer will have a good sense of how your child is going to look under his particular studio lights. If the photographer suggests a little blush or color, then go ahead and use it conservatively. The last thing you want is to have your child looking like a wax doll in his or her photos!

Absolutely, positively, without exception, do not allow your child to wear a white shirt or blouse as one of his or her changes of clothes.

There is always an exception to this rule, but white will not only wash out the photo with bright spots, but also reflect unwanted light all across your child's face as well as wash out some of his or her features. Also, no busy prints or plaids, as these attract the eyes to the pattern and deter from the main focus of the photo—your child! Solids work best. A quick glance through the *Players Directory* will show you that the majority of shirt colors for kids are black and dark solids.

No trendy logos, either. Unless he is Tiger Woods, having a Nike emblem on your child's shirt is a definite no-no. The same goes for Polo shirts and other recognizable logos such as Abercrombie and Fitch. Believe it or not, a solid black T-shirt works wonders. This logo no-no is also true for background performers, which I discuss further in Chapter 8.

Prior to arriving at the photo session, you should have already let the photographer know the kind of photos you want to have taken, but it is a good idea to remind her of the type of photo you are looking for. You might also ask how much she would charge for one more roll of film and proof sheet or a few more photos per change.

During the shoot, the photographer will be talking to your child the entire time. If your child is on the shy side, you may be tempted to answer all the questions yourself. Resist this temptation. The photographer uses these questions and trains of thought to try to elicit certain expressions and a spark from your child. For instance, he may ask where your child is from and upon discovering you are from out of town ask your child if she talks to any of her friends from back home. This can sometimes lead to a sad or sincere photo. Or he might ask if your child has a pet, what her favorite subject or food is, whether she has been to Universal Studios yet, and so on to try to get a good smile.

Following the shoot, thank the photographer, make sure you collect everything you came with, and ask when you will be able to pick up the proof sheet to review. A typical turnaround is three to four days. At that time, go over the proof sheet first with the photographer, as he will have good insights as to which of the photos he thinks turned out the best. If you have an agent, she will also want to look over the sheet. Unless your agent protests, follow the photographer's advice and order up his suggestions for prints. The price you paid for the photo shoot

Landscape headshot of Dylan Patton.

will also give you two to three eight-by-ten prints from the proof sheets. Once these are blown up, you can see flaws that might rule one or more out. Finally, after you decide on the winners, *do not order copies from the photographer!*

The photographer may charge ten dollars per glossy reprint, but there are several reproduction companies in town that will do it for less money and also print the additional information you should have on the photo such as name, contact number, agency, and so on. While glossy photos were once the norm, these days it is much more cost-efficient to use lithographs, or lithos, for your photos. An added benefit of lithos is that they can be run through your laser printer so you can print your child's résumé directly on the back.

There is a new style of headshots appearing in Los Angeles and New York. The new headshots are in black and white or full-color, and fill the entire print. Oftentimes these photographs don't have the name on the front and rely on a résumé to be attached. Please see examples of

Portrait headshot of Emilee Greenberg.

a portrait and a landscape headshot (courtesy FlyGirl Photography) above.

OTHER PHOTOS

As your child's career progresses, there may be a need for one or more additional types of photographs. These include the composite, the three-quarters shot, the full-length shot, and the ZED (or comp) card.

The composite consists of four different photos on one eight-by-ten glossy print. The composite is preferred by commercial casting agents for younger actors because it shows the child in different situations. This is where advanced planning comes in. If you are planning to create a composite, you will most likely need a few props (basketball, glasses, tennis racquet, teddy bear, baseball cap, chemistry set, etc.). Likewise, you will need the appropriate changes of clothing. Since this photo shoot will be more time-intensive for the photographer (waiting for changes, etc.) it will probably cost a little more. This is why communication with your photographer is a must so that expectations are clearly understood.

The three-quarters shot is used mainly in modeling but is gaining in popularity with agents and managers. Contrary to what some actors think, the three-quarters shot has nothing to do with the amount of torso present but rather the angle of the subject in front of the camera. Many photographers will shoot a few three-quarters shots during a standard photo shoot to add to the selection you will choose from.

The full-length shot is simply a photo of your child's full body standing casually. Usually you will see this kind of a shot on a composite with the child wearing some formal wear, overalls, a ballerina tutu, or some other interesting outfit. There really is no need for these at first, and they are hardly used for film and television casting, but it will give an agent or casting director a good, overall view of your child's body type and stature.

The ZED card is actually just a smaller version of a composite photograph printed on a five-by-seven-inch postcard. Since the size is smaller, you should choose only the best photographs to feature on the ZED. ZED cards generally include a headshot with the child's name on the front and then four or five individual photos on the back.

THE RÉSUMÉ

Next to a photo, a résumé is essential to let agents and casting directors know more about your child such as special skills, hobbies, previous experience, training, and awards. You can find a sample résumé on page 29. The résumé should be neatly typed and free of written-in additions as well as contain a valid contact phone number or answering service. For children, it is not essential to list body measurements. It used to be common to list a Social Security number on the résumé itself. With the current rise in identity theft and the selling of photos on online

CULLY SLOAN

The Really Great Talent Agency
5555 Ventura Blvd. #55
Sherman Oaks, CA 91423
(555) 555-1212

Hair: Lt. Brown   Weight: 75 lbs.
Height: 4'8"   Eyes: Brown

FILM:

Revenge of the Stage Moms	Principal	Warner Bros.
Year to Date (*mow*)	Featured	NBC, Nick Shally, Dir.
Losing Face	Lead	Universal Studios

TELEVISION:

Silent Island	Series Regular	Josh Harvey/FOX
Of Swords and Pens	Guest Star	Barbara Klein/CBS
Paper Cut	Boy #1	Julie Kraven/Nickelodeon

AWARDS:

Young Artist Award 2003	Nominee	for *Silent Island*

COMMERCIALS:
Conflicts available upon request

TRAINING:
Scene Study—Bret Potter
Cold Reading—LeAnne Seibert

SPECIAL SKILLS:
Tennis, computers, voice impersonations, skiing, chess, swimming, singing. Can touch tongue to nose.

auction sites, including your child's Social Security number on the résumé is no longer a requirement and should be avoided.

Remember to list only the real credits your child has earned. Hollywood is full of stories of people who lied on their résumés only to have the director of the project they supposedly starred in call their bluff later on. If your child has only local theatre credits, list them under theatre and omit the film and television categories entirely. Focus on his training, if any, and also his special skills, such as baseball, football, ballet, touching his tongue to his nose, and so on. Every little bit under special skills will help the beginning young actor in finding work. When entering information for work done in commercials, rather than list them on the résumé, simply say "Conflicts available by request." If your child has done a commercial for Pepsi and is being considered for a Coca Cola Spot, having that on the résumé may be detrimental.

There is some debate among performers when comparing résumés as to which category a job actually falls under. The most common types of categories that are listed on a theatrical résumé are series regular, co-star, lead, and featured. Many parents like to inflate the importance of a particular role and will put co-star when their child had one line in an ensemble scene. You are free to do this—the résumé police are not going to bang down your door and demand a retraction. However, if you keep your child's résumé modest and more accurate, it will more fully represent her experience and talent for the prospective casting director or producer.

It was once uncommon to use an L.A.-style résumé in the New York theatre scene, but more and more, these walls are coming down, and now the same basic résumé can be used in either place. Just remember to keep it clean, keep it real, and keep on working!

4

Interview with Scott Cox

SCOTT COX IS A YOUNG ACTOR WHO HAS APPEARED IN episodes of *Yes, Dear*; *Jag*; *Just Shoot Me*; and the TV movie *Firestarter 2*. In addition to acting, Scott appeared with the group Gimme 5 on Ed McMahon's *Next Big Star* and is currently pursuing a solo singing career in addition to his acting career.

Q: When did you decide that you wanted to get into the entertainment business?
A: When I was six years old my mom took me to get my pictures taken at a photography studio. They dressed me up in all these different costumes with props: motorcycle guy, businessman, cowboy, et cetera. I guess I "went into character" for each scenario. My mom says that in minutes, I had three photographers working with me and trying to convince her that I should get into the business. She said no and wouldn't even discuss it. I bugged her to death about it, though, until she finally cracked. We made a deal. She told me that I could take acting classes for a year and then if I still wanted to be an actor, we could go for it. After a few months, though, agents came to my class and signed me and I booked my first commercial for Chevy a few weeks later.

Q: What were your first experiences like in Florida?
A: It was so cool; I had a lot of fun mostly doing commercials, but a few TV shows, stage plays, and movies too.

Q: *How did you make the decision to move to California?*
A: Actually a manager from Hollywood came to Florida and asked to meet with my mom and I. He sort of brought us to L.A. and showed us around. We loved it and that first month I got a job, so we stayed.

Q: *Would you have done anything differently in the beginning?*
A: Not really. My mom and I decided that if I was going to go to L.A., I should also try singing too. So I made a demo. Maybe I should've got more experience in that area.

Q: *Is it harder to make friends, and do they treat you any differently?*
A: Yes, mostly because I'm home-schooled. I sort of like to meet girls who don't know what I do. If they find out, sometimes they get all weird about it and change how they act around me. It's really no big deal, but they think it is.

Q: *Do you have any advice for kids just starting out their careers?*
A: Just what I *always* say: "Dreams really *do* come true with lots of hard work and prayers." Oh, one more thing: after you do an audition, forget about it, or it'll drive you nuts. And get used to *many* "no's."

5

CHAPTER

Making the Move

THE DAY WILL EVENTUALLY COME WHEN YOUR CHILD WILL ask when she will be able to make a movie or be on an episode of 7th *Heaven*. This will be a decision that will affect the whole family, so get everybody involved. Choosing to move to Los Angeles or New York to pursue your child's career should be done with the utmost care and sensitivity to what your child needs and wants, as well as your realistic ability to provide it for her.

This decision could be one of the most difficult ones that your family will face. Many parents will pack up their entire families and move everybody right away and worry about finding jobs for one or both parents once they get there. Others will send one parent off with the child and the other will stay behind and work his or her day job until the career gets going and he or she can move out to rejoin the family. There is not one perfect scenario that will magically give you all the answers to this question.

In the entertainment business, timing is everything. If you are trying to get an agent, the best time is in early June through September. Likewise, the time most parents and children who do not live in the Los Angeles area come to town is called pilot season. This is a time that begins in January, when the shows for the new television season are cast and their premiere episode produced. During this time, an agency's office is usually a hive of activity as they are trying to get their existing clients pitched for all of those roles. You can see how they would have little or no time to entertain submissions to join the agency at this time.

January is the time of another big event in Los Angeles; the International Modeling and Talent Association show, or IMTA. This is a week-long event that brings young models and performers to one place where they can showcase their talents and have individual meetings with talent managers from across the country. The event is held twice a year—January in Los Angeles and July in New York City. More information on the IMTA is available at its website at *www.imta.com*.

Most of the kids who move out to Los Angeles for pilot season have accumulated a variety of credits someplace else and are taking the next step in their career by going to where the most action is. If your child is still lacking experience in local commercials and does not yet have an agent, your time would be better served by continuing your child's education and training about the business of acting and approaching agents and managers in your area of the country. Melanie Cox, whose son Scott is a working actor in Los Angeles, did not move to California until after Scott had a hefty list of national and local commercials and two small film roles.

If you are a single parent, it can be a particularly trying experience to uproot yourself and your child and head to the big city. The hard truth is that if you are getting child support in a state with a lower cost of living, more than likely it will not be adjusted when you move to Los Angeles. If you are coming out to Los Angeles for a couple of months during pilot season, a good resource to consult is the Screen Actors Guild. The guild often has information on other parents who are looking for somebody to share the rent in an apartment. Another place that parents and children stay at is the Oakwood Temporary Housing complex, within sight distance of Warner Bros. Studios. Its rates can get pricey, but it also offers seminars and meet-and-greets with other parents.

Another option I see parents do all the time is negotiate with their manager (if they have one) to have their child stay with their manager during pilot season and sometimes longer. While I would like to believe that every manager has the emotional and professional well-being of his client in mind, this type of arrangement is obviously suspect to scrutiny. If you are sending your child to live with your manager for an extended length of time, it goes without saying that both you and your child need to have the utmost trust in the manager. There are wonderful managers who simply may not click with one of their clients on a day-to-day basis. This is expected and natural. It would be a tremendous disservice to put your child in an environment where the primary caregiver was uncomfortable to be around. There has been some talk about a husband and wife from the Chicago area who intend to retire in the L.A. area and are looking into providing a place to stay for young actors and actresses who cannot have their parents with them in the city at all times. While I am not aware of this type of hospice or group home existing yet, it would be a great benefit to families.

If you send your child to live with someone else, you will also need to make sure that you give complete guardianship of your child to that person for the duration of the stay. This will allow the guardian to enroll your child in school (send her records!) and take her to the doctor or dentist and so on.

Moving out to L.A. is not necessarily going to further your child's career any faster than continuing the local work he has already begun to cultivate. In fact, there has been a trend in recent years to go and scout out new talent completely outside of the traditional Hollywood scene. Edward Furlong of *Terminator 2* was raised in Southern California but did not have any acting experience other than a very small part in his fifth-grade play. Like his character in *Terminator 2*, Furlong had a tough life—his mother gave up custody of him at an early age and he lived with his aunt and uncle most of his childhood. He was at the local Boys Club in Pasadena when he was discovered by a casting director who simply asked if he would like to be in a movie. A couple of auditions later, he got the part.

The same casting director that discovered Eddie Furlong later found another star in young Brad Renfro from Tennessee, who was cast as Mark Sway in *The Client*. Like Furlong, Renfro was a streetwise kid who had had family problems and lived with his grandmother. These instances of being discovered are rare but they happen. Joseph Gordon-Levitt of *Third Rock from the Sun* fame has expressed his thoughts on this type of casting numerous times in interviews and speeches. "Let us act—we're actors!" exclaimed Gordon-Levitt at *The Hollywood Reporter's* YoungStar Awards in 1996.

The conversations with your family should remain open and you should treat your child as an equal partner in deciding whether to move out or to give it more time. If you have not taken the step in signing with an agent or manager, I would highly recommend not packing up and heading out West to try to make it or break it. There are good talent agencies and managers spread out across the country that are willing to consider new talent. You can find a list of regional talent agencies in Appendix 2.

When you sit down for your first family meeting to discuss whether or not to relocate to further your child's career, it is also a good time to begin to map out a plan of action for that career. The motion picture business has been around for more than eighty years; it is wise to remember this rather than think you can show up and have people flocking to you for attention and wanting to make your child an overnight success. It's important not only to make goals but to keep them. Chances are at your first family meeting you will decide to keep doing the local scene for the time being. This can be heartbreaking for your child, so explain to her the reasons it would be better to wait.

When setting your goals, it is important to make several small goals rather than start off the bat with "star in a movie with Sylvester Stallone." While that can be one of the top goals in your child's goal pyramid, you should structure your goals so that they are smaller and easily attainable, yet build on each other up to a pinnacle.

When I first moved to L.A. in 1995 I made a similar list:

1. Obtain steady employment so I can pursue my other interests on my own schedule.
2. Attend as many TV sitcom tapings as humanly possible.
3. Try to remember as many names as possible during these tapings.
4. Get into the Internet Movie Database within two years.
5. Get my Screen Actors Guild card.
6. Work as an actor full-time.

As you can see from my example, there were several distinct steps that I went through to attain that goal of working as a full-time actor. Each one built upon itself until steps 4 and 5 fell into place almost by themselves. On a side note, I personally wish I would have followed my own advice about waiting to move and furthering my local résumé first. I am still working on number six—there should always be a higher goal.

A realistic goal pyramid for your child to make while still working at the local level may include

1. Don't be afraid to sing if somebody asks me to.

2. Get a part in the community theatre's annual musical.

3. Do the voice-over for a local commercial.

4. Attend the International Modeling and Talent Association's (IMTA) convention in New York or Los Angeles.

5. Sign with a manager.

6. Sign with an agent.

7. Work as an extra on my favorite TV series.

8. Join the unions.

9. Star in a movie with Sylvester Stallone.

These are all ambitious goals, which may take many smaller steps to accomplish. You can be as detailed as you want working with your child to set them.

I'll talk more about agents, managers, and the unions later in this book. By setting achievable, yet ambitious, goals your child will be able to see that the hard work he is putting forward at the local level is being rewarded. The atmosphere at such a crucial time in your child's life is very important. It is better for him to try out for a play close to home and not get the part he wanted than to be in L.A. away from friends and part of his family and feel rejected, sad, and angry.

If you have your family meeting and things are leaning toward making the move, take each one of those goals that might pertain to the move and break them out into specific steps you are going to work on when you get out there. This process is an important one that I call P and P—planning and partnership. At this stage you must reiterate with your child that the entire family is choosing to support her in her new endeavor. Start talking about where you are going to live, where you and your spouse are going to work. How long will it take to sell your house? Will you be able to take the dog with you? These are all important aspects of uprooting your family.

Earlier I mentioned pilot season, which is the time of year that the networks are trying to produce the next hit TV shows for the upcoming year. Typically pilot season will begin in January and start dropping off in March; however, some networks begin casting and shooting as early as November. For the new actor arriving from out of town, pilot season would be an inappropriate time to begin his career. The best time to relocate to L.A. would be during the summer after his regular school year ends, so he can begin at his new school and work on creating his talents and professional tools to get ready for pilot season in the coming months.

ALL IN A NAME

Choosing whether or not to have your child take on a stage name is a tough decision. While it was once necessary for actors to change their names to avoid religious and ethnic stereotypes and blacklists, today's casting directors and audiences are more tolerant and recognize the contribution of all ethnicities and religious denominations. That being said, however, if your child has a relatively hard to pronounce name, chances are you will hear somebody mention that you should change it.

Approach the topic carefully with both your child and your spouse. For many fathers, the surname given to their children is a sign of pride and a way to continue the lineage to the next generation. There are reasons other than pronunciation that could warrant this discussion. First, there could be another actor with the same name in one of the unions your child is going to be a part of. This is especially true if your child has a common last name such as Smith or Anderson. Another reason is to provide the family with a degree of privacy once your child is in the public eye.

The digital age has provided a way for your family to be tracked from one place to another. Where it used to be that you could simply change your phone number and just worry about out-of-date phone books that listed your address, with the Internet and huge archival databases, chances are that somebody will eventually find out your home address, at the least, and contact you there directly. By creating a stage name for your child, it will still be possible, but more difficult.

The creating of a stage name does not necessarily have to involve both the first name and the surname. When confronted with the necessity of changing their name, many actors opt to simply reverse their middle and first names and go by their middle name professionally. The decision of whether or not to change your child's last name should be a mutual one made by the family.

If you decide to change your child's name to a stage name, obtaining the advice of a lawyer experienced in such matters is always the best course of action. If your child is merely using her middle name instead of her first name, more than likely she will be able to do so without a getting court order and making other arrangements and filings. This is referred to as *common usage* and is along the same lines as Richard going by the name Dick or Michael going by Mike. The main thing to remember in proceeding with a name change is that no matter whether it is common usage or a court-approved name change, the name cannot be changed for fraudulent purposes.

If your child is going for an entirely new name, or perhaps taking his mother's maiden name, you will more than likely need to file several papers and requests to legally change your child's name. Guidelines for a legal name change state that you cannot change a name to that of an established trademark, such as Pepsi. Additionally, numbers are not allowed in a name unless they are Roman numerals after the name. Finally, a legal name cannot contain profanity or racial slurs.

6

CHAPTER

Interview with Melanie Cox

MELANIE IS THE SINGLE MOTHER OF SCOTT COX, WHO HAS co-starred in numerous commercials, TV shows, and pilots and was a member of the singing group Gimme 5. She and Scott live in the Los Angeles area.

Q: How did you know it was time to move to Los Angeles?
A: Scott had already made a name for himself in Florida. He was a big fish in a little pond there. His résumé had about twelve commercials, two TV shows, and two movies on it in just fifteen months' time. Casting directors and agents knew his work and he had a very good reputation. This spread to a manager in Hollywood who was coming to Florida and asked to meet Scott and I. After spending a few hours with him, he convinced us to come to L.A. for the month of July 1989. When we got off the plane, he met us with a *full* itinerary, three to four appointments a day, Monday through Friday, with casting directors, agents, and other representatives in the business. They all told us that if we lived in L.A., Scott would work. If not, there [was] not much they could do for us in Florida. We had our pick of three agents who wanted to sign him across the board and by the end of that month, he had already booked an episode of *Touched by an Angel* for CBS. We went back to Florida, packed up what we could fit into our car and drove out here to live. Scott averaged a job a month, mostly working as

a guest star on episodes of TV shows, along with a few commercials, voice-overs, and films.

Q: What strains does being in the entertainment business put on the family?
A: Everyone's situation is different, but for us, it has been a struggle to stay here in L.A. I closed my child care business in Florida to come here and have found it *very* difficult to find a job that will work around Scott's schedule. I home-school him in the mornings until around 1 P.M., we then run lines for auditions, and sometimes have several auditions or studio sessions for his singing career in the afternoons and don't get home until 7 or 8 P.M. That can be very hard on a marriage also. A man's pride can be hurt when your family is hardly ever home and your child makes more money than you do. Some men can handle it, and some can't, I guess. My husband and I separated.

Q: What is the biggest misconception you have heard or seen when it comes to kids in the biz?
A: There is plenty of talent out there and in L.A. the competition is very tough. My heart goes out to the people who bring their kids out here with no résumé and no experience or training. There are so-called managers who travel around "finding new talent" and convince parents that their kids will do well in Hollywood if they come out and train with them. I have seen so much of this that it breaks my heart. The cost of living here is extremely high and this training is expensive too. So many come here for months trying to get a break, then go home broke and defeated with no success, or maybe they have done a little extra work. This is very hard on the kids! It's much better to build up a résumé with lots of training and local jobs, then branch out gradually.

Q: Does working in an "adult" business cause any specific problems or concerns?
A: When he was younger, I [used to feel] guilty for having to interrupt Scott's playtime to get him ready for an audition, et cetera. However, I have raised a son who was very involved in sports and I also had to interrupt his playtime for practices and games, et cetera. It's really no different. If a kid makes a commitment to be involved in something, it teaches [him] responsibility to see it through. This is totally Scott's choice to do this and you have to take the bad with the good. Now that

he's fourteen, he sometimes wishes that he went to public school for the socialization. I simply tell him that if he wants to cut way back on his singing and acting, he could go to public school. However, he is currently two grade levels ahead, so it would actually be a huge disadvantage to attend public school. I try to keep him involved in lots of activities where he is around kids his own age: church youth group, fencing, dancing, the local community center, and anything else he is interested in. There are lots of resources out there to get your kids involved in.

Q: How can single parents not only support their kids but also provide the basic necessities?

A: My goal as a single mom is to keep Scott happy, healthy, his head on straight, and his feet firmly planted on the ground. I've always told him that if this business changes his personality, no amount of money or fame is worth that and I'll take him out of it! Believe me, he *knows* I would. He's a very sweet, kindhearted, and understanding kid who is quite mature for his age. I really feel that I not only have a great son in Scott but a best friend for life also! We support each other, and he is always there for me as I am [for] him. He can tell when there's something wrong and never fails to try to help me through it, sometimes with just a hug and an "I love you, Mom." He tells me all the time that I'm "the best mom in the world" and no matter what I'm going through, *that* makes it all worthwhile and gives me the strength to carry on.

Q: Do you have any advice for other parents just starting out?

A: My advice to other parents just starting out is to make sure it is in your child's heart to do this, not yours! Get all the training you can and fill up that résumé *before* coming to L.A., and when you come to L.A., sign up for all the training your agent recommends. Listen to your agent's advice. Then your child will have a good chance of booking!

Q: Is there anything you were never told about that you think every parent should know?

A: Parents are greatly in need of information on set etiquette and what is expected of them and their child after they book a job. A "policies and procedures" type of manual should be given to them.

7
CHAPTER

Training in Los Angeles

CONTINUING YOUR CHILD'S TRAINING IN TELEVISION, FILM, and theatre is one of the most important things you need to consider once you are in the Los Angeles area. The area is full of classes and opportunities for training, and weeding out the legitimate classes from the rest of the pack can be a huge task. Before you set out to find the right training for your child, you should carefully consider whether or not your child needs training at this stage in both her physical and mental development as well as her career.

Children under the age of seven or eight can get by in their young careers by using what they have been given naturally. Their sense of wonder and energy can provide them the inspiration needed to fulfill a role in either a film or a commercial. In fact, many acting directors look for that special energy and childlike wonder in casting at this young age rather than any formal training.

As your child gets older, he will be more accustomed to taking classes and attending school and he should be ready to attend a class on acting, modeling, or dancing by the time he is eight or nine years old. At this point your child will also be getting more self-conscious about his performance and appearance, and formal training at this stage can be crucial in letting your child know that it is OK to recognize where he needs help in his performing technique.

Training in the early years of your child's career should be fun. In addition, your child really should not have more than one session a week with an instructor. I have seen parents whisk their child to karate one night, acting lessons the next, Scouts the next, and a voice class after that. Throw in some other sports for school or clubs and you have a very full schedule. One class a week will allow your child to look forward to the next session as well as fully digest what the instructor is trying to teach.

Finding the right instructor for your child will take some time. You can begin with the list on page 45 and also consult the yellow pages in the phone book, ask other parents, and of course consult your agent or manager. When you are looking for a class, the first thing you need to do is contact the school and ask if you and/or your child can attend a class and meet with the instructor prior to signing up. Most classes will allow you and your child to audit a class without paying anything up front. When you attend the class, pay attention to how the teacher interacts with the kids. This is important as your child will need to have a good rapport with the instructor to get the best training as well as your money's worth. If you are watching and waiting with other parents, do not be afraid to ask them questions about the class and the instructor. Finally, on the ride home, talk with your child and ask her what she thought of the class and of the instructor. Going through a list of potential classes will take some time. If you visit one a week, it could take several months before you and your child find an instructor she is comfortable with.

If you are sending out headshots and résumés to casting directors, you may get phone calls and letters from places offering workshops and seminars for actors. They will usually say that somebody currently in their class gave your child's name to them as somebody who might be interested. These are scams! After casting directors throw away headshots and résumés these scam artists pick them out of the trash and go through them. They will call you pretending to be referred by somebody you know, but for privacy reasons cannot tell you who, and try to sell you their class. If you happen to be on the receiving end of such a call, get the caller's phone number and call the Screen Actors Guild immediately to report the scam.

RECOMMENDED INSTRUCTORS AND CLASSES

Young Actors Space
5918 Van Nuys Blvd.
Van Nuys, CA 91401
Phone: (818) 785-7979
Email: *youngactorsspace@pacbell.net*
Web: *www.young-actors-space.com*

The Young Actors Space (YAS) was created in 1979 by Diane Hardin, a veteran of both stage and screen. Together with Nora Eckstein, she has made the YAS the leading training ground for young actors in the Los Angeles area. Some of their past students have included Chad Allen, Lukas Haas, Danny Nucci, Hilary Swank, Jessica Biel, Kirk Cameron, Leonardo DiCaprio, Tobey Maguire, River Phoenix, and Elijah Wood.

Kristopher Kyer Workshop for Actors
850 N. Hollywood Way
Burbank, CA 91505
Phone: (818) 845-5578
Web: *www.kyerworkshop.com*

Kristopher Kyer has been teaching young actors for more than ten years and lends his personal experience to his teachings. Some of the young performers he has coached are Tyler Hoechlin, Joseph Ashton, Scotty Leavenworth, Cole and Dylan Sprouse, and Jessica Simpson.

Kevin McDermott
10170 Culver Blvd., Suite 102
Culver City, CA 90232
Phone: (310) 837-4536
Web: *www.centerstagela.com*

Kevin McDermott was a certified elementary and special education teacher before beginning his successful acting classes at Centerstage L.A. What began more than seventeen years ago has trained hundreds of young actors, several of whom have gone on to be nominated for

Emmy Awards. Kevin and his instructors speak from experience and have been hired as coaches on many different television series.

Weist-Barron-Hill
4300 W. Magnolia Blvd.
Burbank, CA 91505
Phone: (818) 846-5595
Web: *www.wbhactingschool.com*

Michael Woolson Studio
1040 South La Jolla Ave.
Los Angeles, CA 90035
Phone: (323) 933-7133
Web: *www.acting4film.com*

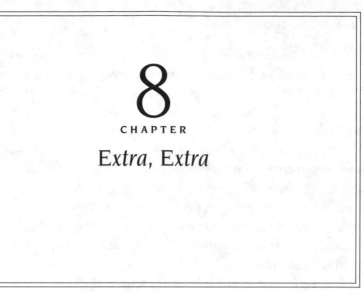

8
CHAPTER

Extra, Extra

ONCE YOUR CHILD IS TRYING TO GET INTO SHOW BUSINESS, you will find yourself noticing more and more things on television and in movies that you may have missed before. You may notice a boom microphone in some of the scenes in a movie theatre, or perhaps you stay longer at a movie to watch the closing credits just to get the name of the assistant director. Another thing you will notice is that if a production included only the main cast of characters in the entire show, it would be a very boring, empty production! In many scenes you will see what seems like hundreds of people in the background of the scene walking along the street, shopping, in the hallways at a school, playing Frisbee in the park, and doing other things. These people you see were not simply in the area when the production company started filming. Each and every one of them is a paid actor with a specific role to fulfill; they are called *background performers*, or the rather unflattering term *extras*.

Background work will not make your child a lot of money, but like everything, it is a way to learn about the business from being around those that are in the business. The background performers on any given production will make anywhere between sixty and one hundred dollars a day depending on whether they are union or nonunion. As you can see, even if a background actor worked every day for the entire month, after taxes and the agent's commission, it would be very difficult to live on that amount. Many actors young and old pursue extra work early in their careers both to see how the business works and with the hope of getting noticed and maybe breaking into the business.

Production companies use a variety of different services when looking for their background actors. In the L.A. area alone there are many different extra casting agencies that fulfill the needs of big and small productions. Many of the smaller agencies will specialize in placing background performers with special abilities or exotic looks. These casting agencies will pretty much represent everybody who fills out their registration form and pays a registration fee.

The biggest background casting agency in the Los Angeles area is a combination of two companies: Cenex Casting, which handles nonunion extras, and Central Casting, which handles union extras. Both of these agencies are mainly for adult background performers or those eighteen-year-olds who can play younger. For children, the background agency most frequently used is called Kids! Background Talent. Kids! is located in Burbank at 207 South Flower Street, between Olive Avenue and Alameda Avenue. Kids! Background Talent charges a registration fee of thirty dollars that covers computer imaging and a photo reproduction fee for your child. In order to register you will need to fill out an application, available on the company's website at *www.extrasmanagement.com*, and submit a copy of your child's Social Security card and of course a valid work permit.

Unlike most talent agencies, background performer agencies will rarely call you directly to let you know something is available. Instead, background placement agencies will use a work line that is updated throughout the day and that you have to check periodically to know what is available. On the recording will be the name and phone number of the agent in charge of the casting call, so you may then talk to him directly. Some casting calls are on the recording for only split seconds, so luck truly plays a part in getting background work. Some background actors who are experienced will hire a call-in service that will make the calls throughout the day for them and will then contact the performer when one of the jobs meets certain criteria. You can find the names and addresses of various call-in services in the yellow pages.

Unlike the lead actors in television shows and feature productions, background performers are expected to dress the part of the character they are playing. Successful background actors have many different costumes in their wardrobe collection. Some even have their cars or minivans decked out with metal rods to hold an ample supply of different ensembles for different occasions. Usually, however, the casting agency will tell you what type of wardrobe will be required for the particular production that your child will be working on. If the agency doesn't let you know, then take two to three changes of regular, clean shirts (no logos), a pair of good jeans, and nice pair of khakis for boys and khaki shorts and several tops for girls.

It may be helpful to look at a hypothetical example of a common call for background performers. Let's take a look at a typical scene for the television show *ER*. The main set for this show is the triage center at a hospital in Chicago. There is a very large waiting room as well as a central area where doctors and nurses crisscross the room, barely missing each other. Beds line the side of the main area and the place is nearly always bustling with activity. If your child is going to be an extra in a hospital scene, what type of costume should she bring to the set? Think about the last time your child was in the emergency room or doctor's office. A clean pair of pajamas is a good suggestion for children through the age of fourteen. A two-piece set for summer and a footed sleeper for winter would be great choices to bring along. For older children, a worn-in T-shirt and sweatpants or sleep pants would fit this costume choice. Another good piece of wardrobe would be jeans with a hole in the knee, suitable for applying special effects makeup to look like a skinned knee. A child-size hospital gown is a good thing to bring if you have it. Other than these, a good standby is your normal, clean-looking clothes that your child might wear to an audition or to school. Bringing a manageable wardrobe for your child while doing background work allows the director to use your child in various scenes, so do not bring just one thing!

One of the reasons I recommend bringing more than one wardrobe change to a production as an extra is that by law, if your child wears more than one change of his own clothing during the day, the production must reimburse you for the extra expense at incrementing rates. For instance, if you bring pajamas for your child for the hospital scene, and later there is a scene in the park in which your child is running around in the grass in a shirt and shorts, then the shirt and shorts would qualify you for a wardrobe bonus for the day.

The way background performers are treated on the set may be off-putting at first, but you have to put everything in perspective and realize that the crew is providing services for many, sometimes hundreds, of background performers at one time. The sheer number of performers means that everything must be carried out efficiently and on a large scale. When you arrive at the location the casting agency gave you, you will be directed to a parking area specifically for background performers. Sometimes this will be a bit of a walk, as the closer spots are given to the principal cast and to the crew. When you arrive, you will check in with one of the assistant directors and will be given your voucher, which will serve as your paperwork for the day. After the vouchers are handed out, you will go to the wardrobe trailer, where the wardrobe assistant will make sure that what your child is wearing is appropriate and maybe give her a prop such as a backpack, a teddy bear, or a button to wear on her shirt. If the wardrobe assistant gives your child anything additional to wear or carry, he will take the voucher for collateral and direct you to the waiting area.

Background performers are not allowed the luxury of having the company makeup artist or stylist do their makeup or style their hair. For this reason, it is a good idea to keep a personal grooming kit in your purse to make touch-ups or a put quick styling flip in your child's hair. Heavy makeup should be avoided and anything more than a dab on acne should be unnecessary. Styling products should be used conservatively and should not make your child's hair look wet or shiny. The best method is to use products such as gel or mousse in the morning and then use a brush later to take the shine out and keep the hold. After you have been checked out by the wardrobe department, another assistant may come by and take a snapshot of your child that will be used for continuity, that is, to provide a visual record of exactly what your child was wearing, which way her hair was parted, and so on. Do not ask for copies—it will just get you an odd look from the assistant.

The wait may seem like an eternity, but eventually the second assistant director will arrive and give you a little background on the scene your child will be in. At the end of his description, the second AD will then lead you and your child to the set and begin to pick out background performers for various parts of the scene. It is important that both you and your child listen carefully so you both know what the expectations are for the scene. Being attentive can earn your child certain perks such as a *bump*, which is a random line or action that is important in the scene.

Kids who goof around or do not listen are rarely given these jewels of opportunity, so the key is to listen and do what the director and AD tells you and your child to do. Unless both you and your child are doing background work together, you will be asked to watch from off-camera and off-set. Keep in mind that you should not be required to be out of sight or sound of your child, just behind the camera.

As an extra, your child shouldn't try to do anything to get noticed. If your child looks at the camera and smiles even once, the production company could simply say you are done for the day and you and your child will be sent on your way. The way to get noticed is not on camera but behind the camera. How well your child takes direction as a background actor will determine the frequency she is used in later scenes that day.

If your child is working the entire time as permitted by law, the production company will provide both a lunch as well as a snack table, commonly referred to as *craft services*, at the location. The studio set has a definite pecking order: background performers will eat after the main cast and crew are finished. In addition, the snack table for background performers is usually marked as such and oftentimes contains much less appetizing goodies. As a parent, make sure your child knows that there is an order to eating and he must wait his turn.

At the end of the day, the AD will let you know your child is done and you can return any props and wardrobe back to the wardrobe trailer. You will receive your child's voucher from the wardrobe department when they have made sure you returned everything. Take the voucher once again to the AD and get it signed and retain your copy. Your child's paycheck will first be sent to the background agency, which will take its cut, and the remaining balance will be sent to you in about a week.

While background work provides a good education and work experience for your child, this type of work is not regularly seen on résumés. In fact, some established performers will do extra work when times are slow and deliberately keep their faces away from the camera so they are not seen. Since background work seldom requires any memorization or lines, very rarely is it worthy of being mentioned on a professional résumé. If your child receives a bump on a production, then by all means list it on a résumé, but list it as "featured" instead of "background." A good résumé with training and local performances is far better than a résumé with a lot of background work.

9

CHAPTER

Agents

HOLLYWOOD ITSELF HAS HAD A FIELD DAY WITH AGENTS. You yourself probably have visions of money-grubbing schmoozers ready to stab people in the back just to get their 10 percent cut of a performer's wages. Or you may picture an agent as someone who sits in the mall signing people up to try to get a showcase fee from unsuspecting parents, leaving children out of work, out of money, and heartbroken. While these situations sometimes occur, they are few and far between. Most agents are hardworking, underpaid, and pulled every which way between casting directors, production companies, performers, and managers.

An agent arranges opportunities for your child to work. That is the simplest and most direct job description you will ever hear for an agent. The question that immediately comes to mind after that statement is, how? An agency can have anywhere from ten to two hundred or more clients per agent. When you think about those numbers it can be staggering. An agent's day is usually spent in meetings, answering phone calls, and organizing submissions to casting directors.

As you can probably imagine by now, a piece of you child's salary will go to the agent. The standard fee for a commercial or theatrical agent is 10 percent of the net salary. If you are becoming concerned about each additional part of the puzzle taking a portion of your child's earnings, you may want to skip ahead to Chapter 14, "Money," for a startling example.

FINDING AN AGENT

Currently, the world of an agent is in turmoil as a result of an agreement not being reached between the Association of Talent Agents and the Screen Actors Guild for commercial contracts. Up until five years ago, it was easy to tell legitimate agencies apart from questionable ones by the designation of "SAG-franchised agency." However, without an agreement there is no true SAG-franchised agent anywhere, although SAG continues to designate agencies as franchised if they agree to abide by SAG policies. It is up to you to do research to find out whether an agency is legitimate or not.

As Melanie Cox mentioned previously, there are companies out there who prey on aspiring young performers and their families. You can spot the questionable agencies by their marketing techniques. If a commercial agent advertises in the local paper classifieds or the coupon mailer, chances are she is a less than ideal agent. Likewise, if a commercial talent agency sets up an event in your local shopping mall and advertises "See if your child has what it takes!" then run the other way. These commercial agencies may in fact book their clients on a local commercial here and there, but chances are you will be hit with surprises later on.

The number one way to tell a scam from a legitimate agent is if the agent charges a fee up front—for anything. At some of the events that I just mentioned, the agent is likely to say, "Plus our $150 photo session," or "You will need to attend our training classes, which cost $150 for a two-hour session, twice a week." Any agency that charges a fee for representing your child or charges a fee for training, photographs, or showcases is not a reputable agent. If in doubt, check with the Better Business Bureau in the county or state that the agency is located in. While an agent can recommend a photographer or classes, he most certainly should never require you to pay a fee or demand that your photographs be done by a certain photographer.

Getting an interview with an agent can occur in a number of different ways. Most agents get the word about new clients from referrals from casting directors or other actors they represent. Another way that actors get an interview with an agent is the agonizing massmailing of headshots and résumés to every agency in the area. But the best way to attract a prospective agent is to let her see your child through school or community plays and performances.

Doing a mass mailing is unfortunately the first alternative available to those who are just getting started in the industry. This shotgun approach consists of either buying or making your own labels for all the different agencies and writing a generic cover letter and sending them out in batches of ten to twenty a week or even a day. Doing a mass mailing is both the easiest and the hardest way to get into an agent's office for an interview. On one hand, it is the easiest in terms of the least resistance. It is easy to simply buy a fourteen-dollar set of labels, stick them on envelopes, fire them off, and forget about it. Many parents start off this way so they do not have to call in favors from friends and colleagues. I offer some advice on handling mass mailings on page 56.

Let me take time out to address the crucial issue of networking. It seems like everybody knows that networking is important, but everybody is also embarrassed to ask a friend or acquaintance for help. To be successful, you need to shed this fear and leave it at home under the doormat. Everywhere you go in Los Angeles, there are people who know somebody who knows somebody, and oftentimes that same type of networking will occur in your hometown as well.

As an example, I received a phone call from my mother one evening in Iowa while I was working at Warner Bros. in Burbank. She said a lady had just come into her place of work and they got to talking. My mother asked the woman where she was from and the woman replied Los Angeles. The conversation shifted and my mother mentioned she had a son working in Los Angeles for Warner Bros. and the woman replied she worked at Warner Bros. also. Remarkably, one of the women I worked with in the Marketing and Advertising Department had family staying at the senior home my mother worked at! It was truly a case of small-world syndrome and a great example of how everybody around you can be a resource.

Some people routinely say it's who you know in the entertainment business as opposed to what you know. While there is the opportunity for people who have zero ties in the industry to enter the business, it is definitely a major advantage to know somebody who knows somebody. So when your child is getting a haircut and the stylist asks what you or your child does, be honest and up front. Maybe he will be able to offer a referral or know somebody who can help in some way.

Another instance of networking I experienced was when I upgraded my computer and bought a new printer. I put an ad on an online classified site for my old inkjet printer and had a response from a woman who worked in Studio City. Seeing as how we lived very close to each other, she came over to first inspect the printer and then pick it up. When she arrived, she inspected the printer and I did a test print sheet for her and then she wrote out a check. As she was leaving she noticed some headshots of my clients in a pile near my desk and she asked what I did. Well, after a short conversation I found out that she was the head of the Bobby Ball agency, a highly respected children's agency! Needless to say whenever I refer somebody to that agency, I always mention in my letter that I was the one she bought the printer from.

It can be difficult to call on favors from friends and family. Even when you get up the nerve to ask somebody for help, the first words out of your mouth will usually be "I hate to be a bother, but . . ." The truth is that networking is essential to both getting into the business as well as surviving in it. Understanding networking is not just a matter of figuring out which of your acquaintances you can take advantage of and to what degree. More importantly, networking exposes you and your child to new people and can also provide some emotional counseling for both of you in the hard times.

Besides a referral from a friend or somebody you know, another way to approach an agent is through a referral from a casting director you have worked with. If your child has tried out for some parts by approaching casting directors directly, be candid with each casting director about still looking for an agent. Even if the casting director does not think your child is right for the part at hand, she may refer your child to an agent she knows anyway. Most agents will say yes to an interview with your child if referred by a casting director they know and respect. After all, it is the casting director who makes the decision whether or not to employ the agent's clients!

Because many agents feel that they are obligated to see prospective clients referred to them through a casting director, many agents will honor the meeting but be less enthusiastic than they might be with clients they schedule for interviews themselves. That being said, agents are receptive to referrals from casting directors as it helps narrow down their prospective client list based on the reputation of the casting director. This is an important point because there are some people who call themselves casting directors who very rarely perform the duties of a legitimate casting director. If you approach a casting director and he wants a fee to refer you to an agent, that is a pretty good indication to run away and keep one hand on your pocketbook and the other hand around your child's shoulders.

The best way to get an interview with an agent is to have the agent initiate the meeting as a result of seeing your child in a performance. The performance I am talking about does not necessarily have to be something on television or the latest and greatest film; it can also be something as simple as a school or community play. Agents are always on the lookout for new talent and attend performances throughout the community. This is one of the reasons for your child to stay involved in amateur productions while she is looking to turn professional. Not only are school and community theatre productions a great learning experience, but they also provide a way to be seen by agents, friends, family, people who know people, and more.

MASS MAILINGS

As I mentioned earlier, the least effective way to approach an agent is often the first one that parents will try, but they are often quickly discouraged by the results. In fact, even adult actors with stars in their eyes return to this method time and time again and quickly run out of patience and money. This method is tedious, but does often yield results. If you look on the Internet and do a search for "talent agency mailing labels," you will find hundreds if not thousands of different websites that are selling labels of agents' addresses either preprinted or formatted nicely to help the aspiring actor get an interview with an agent—for a modest fee, of course.

A mass mailing of headshots and résumés is not always a money sink, and it can produce results. However, to get results from a mass mailing takes time, patience, and documentation to increase the odds that your child's photo won't simply end up in the circular file or on eBay®. If you are planning a mass-mailing campaign for your child, the number one thing you should remember is that the job is not complete when you drop off those envelopes at the post office. It will take a great number of follow-ups and time to make the most of the submissions your are sending out blindly.

The first thing you should do in preparing your mass mailing is to call the agency you are submitting to and ask for the name of the person in charge of the youth department. If they say they do not have a youth department, ask if they represent children at all. If they say no, then you have just saved money on a submission that would have been thrown away as soon as it was opened. Getting the name of the head of the children's theatrical or commercial department at an agency will allow you to personalize your submission for the agent. In fact, if your mailing label just says "Coast to Coast Talent" and you call up and learn the agent's name is Meredith Fine, I would throw out that label and make up your own, putting the agent's name directly under the agency's name.

The personal touch is very important when contacting an agent, as agents receive hundreds of submissions a day from parents like you. Think of the mail you receive that simply says "Resident"—if you are like many busy individuals, you know right where those letters go! But if a letter has your actual name on it, I bet you give it a lot more time and attention. The same is true with agents. A correctly directed submission is more likely to be opened and considered than one that is addressed to the agency in general.

There are several ways to find an agent in your area that represents children. I have included two lists of well-known agencies that have good child actor departments in Appendixes 1 and 2. Appendix 1 lists agencies in the Los Angeles area and Appendix 2 lists agents in other specific parts of the country. You can find an exhaustive list of franchised talent agents either on the Screen Actors Guild's website at *www.sag.com* or by visiting its office in Los Angeles.

Along with a résumé and a photograph, you will need a cover letter that both introduces your child and tells the agent what type of representation you are seeking for him. An example of a cover letter follows.

Dear [name of agent—you did find it out, right?],

My [son/daughter], [name], is currently seeking [theatrical/commercial] representation in the [city where you live or are looking] area. [He/She] has recently been performing at [name of community theatre], where [he/she] played the role of [role] in the production of [name of production].

We would very much like to speak with you regarding representation with your agency and can be reached at [phone number] or [alternate phone number]. Thank you for your time and consideration.

Sincerely,

[your name]

There are several things to notice in this example cover letter. First, you refer to the agent by name right away. Second, you specifically ask the agent's consideration for representation in either the theatrical or the commercial department. Theatrical is generally considered television and film roles, whereas the commercial department deals mainly with commercials and print work. Some agents oversee both departments while some may specialize and split representation with somebody else in the company. It is also possible for you to have one agency represent you commercially and another entirely theatrically. For now, I would focus on an agency that will represent you unilaterally across the board rather than in one of the individual markets. Be sure to mention both departments if you are looking for representation across the board.

The third thing mentioned in your cover letter is the all-important "what has your child done lately?" section. Here is the place where you can briefly tell the agent about the role your child had in the school or community play. If your child is just starting out, go ahead and list any training your child may be taking and with whom. The performance history you mention should be brief and to the point—this is not the time to try to wow the agent with a complete history of what your child has done—so list only the most recent role. Keep it short and sweet.

Last and certainly not least, provide adequate contact information for the agent so she can get in touch with you. At a minimum this should include your home phone number, but it can also include a cellular phone number, pager number, fax number, and email address. It is not necessary in your cover letter to include your child's Social Security number or a copy of your child's work permit.

Only include your demo tape or compact disc if you are specifically seeking voice-over representation at an agency that has voice-over clients. Including a tape in every package you send out will not only cost you more for the tapes or CDs but also increase your postage fees. Some parents looking for agents for their child include an $8\frac{1}{2}$-by-11-inch self-addressed stamped envelope (SASE) inside each package for the agent to return the photo if she or he is not interested. These tend to have less than spectacular results, so if you must include an SASE, a regular number ten business envelope will do if you are trying to get some kind of response from the agent.

I recommend sending your packages out to agents ten at a time. You should make a list either on a computer spreadsheet like Microsoft® Excel or on a piece of notebook paper that shows to whom you sent packages and the date you sent them. Keep room for additional columns such as Follow-up 1, Follow-up 2, and Follow-up 3. The last column should be a place to write a description about any response you might receive. Keeping track of your submissions serves many purposes including making sure you don't send to the same agent twice in a short period of time, as well as helping you schedule follow-up letters and phone calls.

The time to wait before writing a follow-up varies depending on what your child has been doing since the first letter was mailed out. Many parents mistakenly think the follow-up is merely another letter asking for an interview and making sure the agent received your child's résumé and photograph. Parents who go down that road seldom meet with positive results and instead are simply wasting more postage. A follow-up letter should be sent to agents to let them know when your child has something new of interest that furthers his career.

If your child has the new part of Peter Pan or Wendy in the community play, mention it. More importantly, if your child has been on a professional audition and received a callback, you should start your letter with that information. Callbacks show progress; saying your child is still auditioning and taking lessons from a local teacher does not. Some parents think that only those auditions that end in a job are worthy enough to be mentioned. This is absolutely not true. Callbacks let the agent know that your child is getting noticed and is on the edge of booking a real job.

As mentioned in the section on résumés in Chapter 3, it is important that you tell the truth when contacting agents in both the initial mailing and your follow-up letters. There is nothing more embarrassing than being in front of a prospective agent and having him ask your child, "So what was the callback on Yummy O's like?" only to be met with a blank stare. The small-world concept discussed earlier is equally in place at the agency level and agents have a good feeling of what is made up and what is true. Do your child and yourself a favor and be truthful in all of your correspondence with agents.

It is possible you will be sending out follow-ups to some of the agents you previously contacted at the same time you are sending out your first correspondence to others. You should amend your cover letter for first-time submissions to likewise reflect the callbacks and other performances. Then, the cycle continues as you follow up and send out your next batches and so on. Many parents who are getting discouraged ask, "When will I hear something back?" The three possible answers are soon, later, and never. Chances are if an agent is not interested at this time, you will receive no answer whatsoever. Another response may be that the agent is currently not taking on more clients but will keep your information in her files. (Note: These are the best ones to send your callback follow-ups to!) The best answer is a phone call to set up an interview for your child. Congratulations—next comes the agent interview.

THE AGENT INTERVIEW

If an agent is interested in representing your child, he will contact you or your personal manager to set up a time to come in and meet with your child. It goes without saying, but make sure your child gets plenty of rest the night before and that she has a good breakfast and lunch, depending on the time of the interview. Plan your route out ahead of time to make sure that you arrive five to ten minutes early. If the agency uses a parking structure, be sure to bring enough money to pay for parking; do not expect there to be parking validation.

Do not stress out about what your child will wear to the audition. Clothing should be comfortable, clean, and age-appropriate. It is not necessary to put on your child's Sunday best for the interview, so leave the suits for boys and Snow White dresses for girls at home. A good rule of thumb for children is to dress for auditions the same way they would dress for their school pictures. Simple and nice. You will also want to bring a couple of extra photographs of your child just in case, as well as a snack just in case.

As your child's career progresses and he gets older, he will probably need to prepare a short piece of material he can perform for prospective agents and sometimes casting directors. The agents may want to see your child give a short performance, but she will usually have a script of her own for your child to read from.

Preparing your child for her first agent interview can be tough. It will be a stressful time for you, and that can be readily sensed by your child. The best way to look at an agent interview is to tell your child she is going to simply go talk to an agent. When you arrive in the agent's office you will realize how true that really is. The secretary or assistant will ask you to check in, which usually consists of a sign-in sheet where you will list your child's name and your contact phone number. At an audition for an agent, the agent usually calls your child into his office to conduct the interview without you. This can be scary for children who are just starting out; after all, they have been taught not to talk to strangers and now you are sending them into a room with two or three of them! The anxiety is normal and you should anticipate it and inform your child about what will go on when she is away from you for a little bit.

Once inside, the agent or group of agents will start off by asking your child her name and then some questions about her to loosen her up and to get her talking. This is where the agents can see if your child is mature and open enough to follow directions on set as well. Once they have broken the ice, most agents will then hand your child a section of a script and ask her to read it. This is known as a *cold reading* and it has been known to strike fear into even the most experienced performers. A cold reading is a way an agent can determine the reading level of your child as well as her ability to put feeling into what she is reading the very first time. On a real film or television series, the script can often change several times during filming, so a cold reading can help the agent determine how well your child can read, comprehend, and perform a script she has never seen or heard before.

When the agent is done interviewing your child, you may be asked to join them in the office, where you will be the subject of the next interview. With kids, an agent is looking for the energy and easiness that a child has, as well as ambition for the business. It is very easy to see, especially when your child is alone, if the child is there because he wants to be, or if a parent is pushing him along the whole way. Likewise, when an agent talks with a parent about her child's career, the agent is again trying to see what the motivation is to have the child in the business. The agent will probably ask you about your family. Be honest. If you are single mother with no job and are piggybacking on your child's success, simply say you are a single mother. The last thing you want to be caught in is a lie.

Once your meeting is over, ask if you can leave another headshot with the agent and make sure both you and your child thank the agent and shake his hand on the way out. Oftentimes when a parent hears "Thank you for coming," all of a sudden doubt and disappointment set in and her face almost droops off its bones. Do not expect your child to be offered a contract then and there, although it does happen. Remain confident. When you leave the office, be sure to give your child a hug and compliment him on a great job. Now would be the perfect time for that snack you packed!

Waiting for the response to an agent interview can be stressful, so continue sending out résumés and headshot packages to other agents on your list. If an agent wants to represent your child, she will give you a contract that you will need to look over carefully. Agency contracts are regulated so that agents can take only a 10 percent commission out of your child's pay. In addition, there should not be any agency fee included to add you to the agent's client list. If any agent asks you for money to sign your child, run away! Then call the Screen Actors Guild to inform it about the agency's practices.

Another section of the contract to look at carefully is the section that deals with termination of representation. This clause allows either party to cancel the contract after a certain period of time. For instance, most contracts will allow you to cancel the agreement in writing after three or four months if the agent has not actively tried to get you work in that time. This does not mean that your child has to actually get a part. The agent has done her job if she gets your child an audition; she has no control over how well your child performs at the audition or whether your child is exactly what the producers are looking for.

If you do not hear anything within a week, a follow-up letter is always a good idea. A short letter thanking the agent for meeting with you and your child will suffice. And, of course, if your child has had any callbacks during that time, it is another opportunity to let the agent know. Following up with agents with whom your child has had an interview can be done for months or years if your child consistently has more callbacks and roles in productions the agent can attend. The spreadsheet that details your letters to the various agents comes in very handy here—use it!

WHAT TO EXPECT

The relationship between a client and an agent is one of a professional, mutual understanding on behalf of all parties involved. Since you act on behalf of your child, the agent will also assume you are doing your part of the business duties as well. An agent tries to get your child auditions by sending out your child's headshot and résumé to casting directors. An agent receives breakdowns that describe in very specific terms what type of actor a production is seeking. The agent will send your child on an audition only if she matches the requirements in the breakdown, so sometimes you may feel like your agent is not sending your child out enough. This can be especially frustrating if another child you know in the same agency *did* get sent on a particular audition and your child didn't. There is probably a good reason for this, so it's best to simply forget about it. Perhaps the audition called for a particular special talent such as unicycling or juggling that your child did not have. It is impossible to second-guess the reasons for sending one child out and not another, and questioning the agent will only build bad feelings.

Many parents new to the business ask if it is OK to call your agent. The resounding answer is *yes*. Just don't expect to get through all of the time. A typical day at a busy agency consists of meetings in the morning followed by lunch and then gathering submissions for casting directors in the afternoon. The best time to call your agent is midafternoon after lunch. Be sure to have a reason and purpose for calling so your agent can answer your questions promptly and return to his business—finding your child work!

There are two main reasons that people leave their current agencies and entertain the offers of another. First, once your child starts booking jobs regularly, she may be wooed by larger agencies with more perceived power than the one your child is currently with. Another reason is that you may simply feel that your child is not receiving the amount of attention she should or that she is not being sent out on enough auditions. As mentioned earlier, the key to avoiding bad feelings is to be open with your agent and let him know what you are feeling. While your child may not be going out on many interviews, your agent may be doing all he can at the moment and maybe the jobs just are not there. If your agent has not been able to get your child an audition in three months, there is a clause in most agency contracts allowing you to cancel the relationship immediately.

By far the most stressful reason to leave your agent is because your child has been approached by a larger agency that has a bigger name in the industry than the agency your child is currently with. The new agency may start by sending a letter, and then somehow sporting event tickets appear in your personal mailbox at home, followed by a phone call from one of the agency's more popular performers. Soon they have invited you to meet with the agents and you get the presidential treatment. The fact of the matter is, just because an agency is bigger and seems more powerful, it may not be the best direction for your child to go in. Moving from a small agency through which your child is steadily booking work to a larger agency where she may not be first on the totem pole can be difficult. Many parents and performers find themselves stuck with the larger agency after the newness wears off and they realize the child is not working as much as she did before. To save the embarrassment of going from a large agency back to a small one, many simply stay with the larger agency, hoping things will get better.

Whether or not you decide to move your child to another agency will be a tough decision for everybody. Your agent knows and understands that people will move on at some point in their career, but it's always a painful experience, especially if the agent thinks the relationship is going well. Your child may have also formed a bond with those at his current agency, so suddenly switching to a whole new set of people to get to know can be frightening and overwhelming. Be sure to think the decision through and list the pros and cons for switching agencies. If your pro list is short, then stick it out with your current agent for a little longer. You may also make the decision to let your current agent know that you are being sought after by the other agencies. This can have negative effects on the relationship, but oftentimes it will bring out an expanded dialogue between you and the agent through which she will see your child's importance to the agency.

10

CHAPTER

Personal Managers

FOR MANY PARENTS STARTING OUT, THE THOUGHT OF GIVING away another 10 to 20 percent of your child's earnings to yet another person may seem like a waste. However, like agents, personal managers serve an important function when it comes to supervising and planning the careers of young performers. When starting out down the road of a career, it is indeed possible to serve as your child's manager. To do so effectively, you need to know what managers actually do and ways that a manager can help your child's career move in the right direction.

If you are acting as your child's personal manager, put it in writing. In Appendix 6 you will find a sample manager's contract that you can use and fill out to make it official. It may seem rather redundant signing your name on both the parent's line as well as on the manager's line, but doing so will let your child know that the business relationship with his parent is established and in force.

One of the reasons that some parents choose to manage their child's career is so they can legally use 15 percent of the child's earnings to provide themselves with a salary. While this is done all the time, there are several issues a parent should be aware of. First, the tendency to stray from the best needs of the child are very strong and can easily overwhelm a family who is struggling financially. Many parents may start off doing what they feel is the right thing, such as reinvesting or putting aside the 15 percent they collect as a manager, but too often a family emergency will arise and quickly whittle away the money that has been saved.

Others may decide to be their child's personal manager as a result of hearing stories about other managers and thinking they can do it better than somebody who does not fully understand their child. Whatever the reason you want to become your child's manager, you need to understand that being a personal manager does not simply entail making sure your child gets to an audition on time or gets the latest video game machine in her trailer. It will take good judgment, perseverance, and determination on your part as well as an ability to use basic accounting practices to manage your child's finances.

Hollywood is littered with stories of young performers suing their parents over money they claim their parents took from them. Oftentimes the stories burst onto the headlines from families that have long been considered the perfect family in the press, such as the story about Aaron Carter, brother of Backstreet Boy Nick Carter. In late 2003, Aaron Carter filed a lawsuit alleging that his mother, who appeared on several of Aaron's DVDs and videos, took more than a hundred thousand dollars of his money over the course of several years during which she acted as his manager. He has since dropped the allegations; however, Aaron's family continues to have personal problems. Aaron Carter is far from alone in this feeling. From Jackie Coogan to Macaulay Culkin and now to Aaron Carter, scandals over a child's "fortunes" continue to make the tabloids and celebrity gossip shows.

Acting as your child's manager may be an OK alternative when your child is starting out. During this time you will be coordinating your child's photo shoot for his headshot and/or composite photographs, typesetting his résumé, and of course trying to find an agent so that your child actually gets work. To avoid problems down the road, you should keep ample documentation of expenditures that your child's career entails. This will also help you at tax time. Many parents keep the finances a secret from their child because they think the child will worry too much. Let me assure you, whether or not you include the child in on the discussions about where the money goes, the child will usually worry no matter what, especially if you are in a single-parent household.

For the very young performer, from birth to age six, acting as your child's personal manager can sometimes seem mindless. Do not let the experience at this age affect how you handle her career in later years. Babies and toddlers will get work just by being cute and well tempered. However, as your child gets older, it will depend more and more on your child's ability to follow directions, read, and perform. For this reason, many parents will manage their child's career until age seven or eight and then look to hire a more experienced personal manager. This is perfectly fine and does not reflect negatively on you. You are in charge of providing the best opportunity for your child to succeed in the business.

Many parents find it easier to manage finances if they actually start a business for managing their child's career. By filling out the right paperwork with the city and state, you can create a limited-liability company for your management efforts that will serve to further separate your management business and your family income. All money you receive through the 15 percent manager's fee should be put in this special account. Since it will be an official business, treat it as such. If you take a Hollywood bigwig out to lunch or dinner on behalf of your child, pay for it out of the special account and bill it back to your child. You can then claim it on your business taxes, or your child's taxes.

I cannot overemphasize how important it is that if you are acting as your child's manager, you'd better act like it. However redundant that may seem, simply saying you are a manager and taking the 15 percent is bound to land you in trouble at some point—either with the IRS or with a future lawsuit from your child.

You may be thinking that the role of a personal manager is sounding less like someone guiding your child's career and more like an accountant. Hooray! You've got it. The personal manager oversees the entire scope of your child's career. This includes his finances and keeping track of when a production company makes a deposit into your child's trust account, as well as handling unforeseen emergencies that may require a loan from the bank and other financial matters.

A good financial software program such as Quicken® or Microsoft® Money will help you keep all income and expenses categorized in the right place. As your child gets older, it will also help her learn where the money goes and help her learn the basics about money that every kid should know whether in the entertainment industry or not. Being able to set a budget and plan expenses in advance is a skill that comes naturally for some people and not for others. Today's financial computer programs allow you to enter known income and expenses days, weeks, or even years in advance so you know exactly where the money is going and how much.

A professional personal manager can be instrumental in getting your child an interview with talent agencies. A personal manager is well connected in the business through a variety of agents and you will have a better shot at getting an interview with an agent if your manager can set up the initial interview than you would by simply mass mailing headshots and résumés. Because a personal manager generally has fewer clients than an agent, the manager will spend more time with a new client, getting her ready to interview with an agent. Both this preparation and the reference of a manager will give your child a head start at getting into that agency.

A personal manager generally receives 15 percent of a client's earnings, just as you would if you managed your child's career; however, the percentage sometimes will go as high as 20 percent plus expenses. The percentage can vary from manager to manager, and the expenses they ask to be compensated for can vary as well. Most managers will bill you for any toll calls either to you or placed on your behalf. For this reason, it is a good idea to call your manager back if it is a toll call or have him call you collect if he is out of your local calling area.

Your manager will also request the power of attorney, which means that she will be able to bind you legally into an agreement, as well as collect your salary before passing it on to you. Many parents feel frustrated and trapped by this clause of a management contract, but it is standard practice for personal managers. In agreeing to this, you are also giving the personal manager the ability to do what you are paying her for—managing your child's career and finances. From paying for those five hundred new headshot reprints to making sure your child's acting coach is paid, the personal manager will make sure bills and obligations are taken care of and accounted for.

A personal manager will work closely with you and your child to realize your child's full potential. At the beginning stage this will mean assessing your child's weaknesses and strengths and working to maximize the strengths and working to improve what he needs help with. Your manager will also work with you to have your child's headshots and other photos taken as well as make suggestions for attire and strategies for auditioning, whether for agents or for casting directors. A personal manager is also a friend, someone whom you should trust to work in the best interests of your child and to make overall career decisions. Managers are able to see the long-term benefits or detriments of maintaining roles that may stereotype your child as the whiney brat in films or, like in the Michael J. Fox film *Life with Mikey*, the Cereal King. Through talks with you and your child, the manager will help build your child's confidence and help his personality shine at auditions and on film.

Aside from costs incurred as part of the business, a personal manager will get paid her 15 percent cut if and only if your child books a part. This is yet another reason that the personal manager will work closely with you and your child to ensure that he is receiving the proper coaching and attention he requires to be his best. It is because of this one-on-one attention with the manager that managers sometimes feel like an extended part of the family. However, do not solely rely on the manager to transport your child to and from auditions and/or the workplace. While a manager might show up to an audition or two here and there, it is up to you to make the necessary arrangements for your child.

As was mentioned previously, managers and agents get paid only when your child works. A manager will not submit your child directly for any part that is being cast, but she may stay on top of your agent if she knows your child would fit a particular part that is taking submissions. Many managers also get breakdowns.

Like any decision you have made thus far in your child's career, the decision as to when or if you need a personal manager must be made by weighing all the benefits and looking at your current situation. Bob Jamieson of Noble Media Group suggests, "You should have a personal manager when you are just starting out, or if you already have an agent, you should get a personal manager next. The right time really depends on how involved the parents want to be in their child's career. A manager will help you get an agent, wear the right clothes to a photo shoot and auditions, and guide your child's career. If you are going into the business, find a personal manager as soon as you can."

You can find a list of personal managers by consulting one of the many publications available at the Samuel French bookstore on

Ventura Boulevard in Studio City. You can also find mailing labels on the Internet by searching for "talent manager labels." In approaching a manager, be sure to include a close-up of your child as well as a full body shot. If you are approaching a manager in Los Angeles before you make the permanent move to the area, you can feel free to use the same snapshots you have been using for your local work. If you are already established in Los Angeles, chances are you have already had a professional headshot taken and can include the headshot and some candid photographs in your package. You should also include a short note with the photographs explaining you are seeking a personal manager for your child and what, if any, previous credits, plays, and training your child has had. Because managers have fewer clients than agents do, they oftentimes get too many submissions to handle at any given time. Please be respectful and do not call or email the managers to ask what the status of your submission is. If you do not get a response in a couple of weeks, submit to the next manager on your list.

Unfortunately, talent managers are generally unregulated in the business and not overseen by a general authority. There is an organization called the Association of Talent Managers that is a good start in determining the legitimacy of a personal manager, but the association is a loose one and includes members who simply pay their dues. The lack of regulation has led to a variety of talent managers who will sign on anybody they can in hopes that just one of their clients will prove to be a worthy investment. It is imperative that you investigate and interview with managers who you feel will be good for your child. Talk with other parents or ask some of the folks at the Screen Actors Guild Young Performers Committee if they have heard about a particular manager or if they have any suggestions. You can find more information on the Young Performers Committee in Chapter 16, "Other Resources."

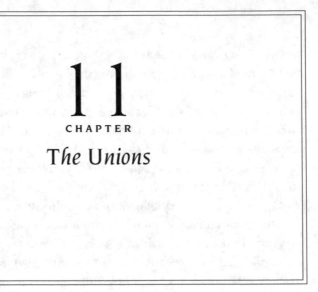

11
CHAPTER

The Unions

IN RECENT YEARS THE UNIONS GOVERNING PERFORMERS IN the United States have become a spectacle in and of themselves. In the past few years we have seen a strike by the Screen Actors Guild, as well as a failed consolidation plan to merge the two largest unions, the Screen Actors Guild (SAG) and the American Federation of Television and Radio Artists (AFTRA).

With all of the headlines surrounding the unions, it is easy to assume that they are a necessary staple to getting your child's career off on the right foot. Many parents join a union too early, assuming that sooner is better. This assumption is oftentimes false and could actually hurt your child's chances of succeeding in larger markets down the road. Joining the unions too early could mean your child would miss out on a great non-union project.

There is absolutely no requirement that your child join one of the performers unions before looking for work in Los Angeles, New York, or your local market. If your child has what the casting director is looking for, he will be able to get the paperwork done for your child to join the union during or after the particular production is finished. Both SAG and AFTRA have a clause in their membership requirements that allows up to thirty days of work on a union production before the performer is required to join the union.

So when should your child join the union? There are conflicting schools of thought on this issue and I myself seem to take both sides depending on the situation. On one hand, it makes sense that the best time to approach the unions about joining is when your child has booked a role and must join. On the other hand, many people suggest joining the union at the first opportunity so that your child is covered by the union's regulations. If your child ever does professional work, he will be required to join the union within thirty days after he has worked on a union project, which is almost all of the professional TV/Film projects.

The best time that I have seen to join one of the performing unions is not until after your child has managed to find an agent and is steadily booking work. This should have allowed you time to decide if show business is something your child is going to continue in, as well as time to save up the necessary initiation fees. As with the many reasons to join the union, there are also several reasons that the best decision may be to postpone joining a union until it is required. First, the initiation fees of the unions are cost-prohibitive to a family who is booking work, much less those who are just starting out. Second, once you join the union, you are bound by the rules of the union, this includes the infamous Global Rule One: no nonunion work. Once you join the union there is little chance that your child will be able to be involved in many smaller productions including student films and other nonunion work. Sometimes the lesser independent films offer a valuable learning experience, but being union, your child would not be able to participate in these projects.

Now that you are more comfortable with the generalities of what a union is and when you should have your child join, we can take a look at the two major representation unions.

SCREEN ACTORS GUILD

The Screen Actors Guild was started in 1933 and was conceived in order to bring a unity of voice among all performers. SAG currently boasts more than one hundred thousand active members and is considered the most powerful actors union in the world. In addition to providing benefits to its members such as health insurance, pension plans, a credit union, and free seminars and classes, SAG exists to protect the rights of its members. Some of the things that SAG does on a daily basis are negotiate contracts between actors, agents, and signatory production companies, as well as maintain certain standards for working on a set such as mealtimes, privacy and wardrobe-changing facilities, and safety. For the young performer, SAG has established even stricter regulations that production companies must uphold. These are discussed more in depth in Chapter 13, "The Jobs."

There are several ways your child can join the Screen Actors Guild. The first is to have a principal role on a signatory production. This simply means having a show that falls under the guild's jurisdiction. A principal role is a part on the show that is included in the cast credits either in the beginning or at the end of the show. You then fill out a form at the SAG office and submit the initiation fee. The current fee for Los Angeles residents is $1,356.00 and the guild does not accept checks.

Another way that performers join SAG is when they are being considered for a major role. This alternative can be difficult to understand at first. Basically, it allows the production company to get the actor into the guild before principal photography begins. This is by no means necessary, as any production can get a waiver called a *Taft-Hartley* to allow the actor to work as a union member before she joins.

Until recently it was also possible to join SAG by working as a union extra, or background performer, for three days. Receiving approval from its members, however, SAG has discontinued that voucher system and is currently reworking the joining requirements for background performers.

AFTRA

AFTRA is the union that has historically represented performers appearing on live television, radio, musical recordings, and news broadcasts. It used to be far easier to determine the jurisdiction a performer fell under by simply knowing that SAG is film and AFTRA is videotape. However, with some television shows being shot on film, and now some films being shot digitally, the two unions sometimes mutually oversee videotaped shows.

AFTRA is probably the easiest of any of the unions to join, which is why many performers young and old join AFTRA first. You simply make an appointment at an AFTRA office, fill out the paperwork, and pay the initiation fee of $1,300.00 and the first six months of your dues.

12

CHAPTER

The Audition

AN AUDITION IS WHEN YOUR CHILD MEETS WITH THE CAST director and sometimes the directors and producers of the commercial, show, or film that needs casting. Your child will usually receive audition appointments through your agent, although it is possible that a casting notice might come to your attention in other ways.

Talent agencies receive what are called breakdowns, which contain specific information about what a particular production or commercial is looking for. An example might read:

"WALK IN THE PARK"

1-Hour Pilot, NBC Studios
Executive Producer: Mark Bannett
Director: TBA
Writer: Aaron Thiel
Casting Director: Adele Miranda
Start Date: TBA
Location: L.A.

WRITTEN SUBMISSIONS ONLY TO:

"Walk in the Park"
Adele Casting Co.
800 South Floral St., Suite 430
Burbank, CA 91502

[JOSEPH ENGEL] A Caucasian man, 30–40, who is an LAPD officer. Joseph's partner was killed while on patrol six months prior. As a result of his mental examination, he has been placed on airport security until the department is satisfied he is mentally capable of resuming his former duties. He is separated from his wife, NORA ENGEL, and they have one child, RALPH ENGEL. *Looking for offbeat character actor with dramatic and comic abilities. Series regular.*

[RALPH ENGEL] Male, Caucasian, age 10–13. Prefer 13–15 to play younger (must look 10–13). Emancipated or GED fulfilled preferred. Son of JOSEPH ENGEL. Slightly overweight and independent child with quick wit. *Recurring.*

The agents in a particular agency will then usually meet to discuss who they want to send out on these auditions and make up a package containing headshots and résumés to send to the casting directors. Breakdowns are a service that usually only agents have access to, simply because of their cost. In fact, the company that puts out the breakdowns, called Breakdown Services, will often list bogus casting notices in their breakdowns and then double-check against their records to make sure that additional copies of the breakdowns are not being distributed illegally.

Breakdowns are not released to actors, and the publisher of the breakdowns will not allow individuals or a group of actors to subscribe to the service. Acquiring breakdowns through any other means is illegal and something the publisher, as well as agents and managers, takes very seriously.

If a casting director would like to see your child for a part, he will contact your agent and let her know when your child should appear for his audition. Once you receive a call from your agent about the specific time, it is a good idea to let your personal manager know, if you have one, and to write down all the specifics in a safe place.

BEFORE THE AUDITION

The word *audition* tends to invoke fear in both children as well as the parents of young performers. There are several things that you can do to make sure that the experience is less stressful on everybody. The key word is *planning*. First, when you get an audition time from your agent, be sure to check to see where the audition is. Los Angeles and the surrounding areas can be a confusing place for even those that have lived there for a while. A good thing to have at all times is a copy of the *Thomas Guide,* a detailed set of maps that includes various counties such as Los Angeles and Ventura. These maps will help you distinguish the distance between appointments if you have more than one on the same day. For instance, just because you have two auditions on Ventura Boulevard does not mean they are within five minutes of each other.

Knowing exactly where the audition is also helps you determine whether two auditions on the same day are workable or if you need to try to reschedule. Keep in mind that auditions can take anywhere from ten minutes to several hours, so it is best to keep one appointment in midmorning and one in midafternoon if possible. If you need to reschedule an audition because you think you won't be able to get there in time, let your agent know immediately and she can try to work something out with the casting director.

Different types of auditions call for different wardrobe approaches for your child. In most cases, solid colors without identifiable brand labels tend to work best for both girls and boys. For a commercial audition, you can bring a bag of props if you like (e.g., glasses, a white doctor's lab coat, etc.) if you think they may come in handy. There are mixed feelings about whether or not these types of gimmicks help or hinder a child's hiring for parts, but there are success stories either way. Use your own judgment and make any props relevant to the product being auditioned for.

There is a trick that many parents do that will help put your mind at ease, especially after you have a few auditions under your belt. Buy an instant camera. Why? At the audition, the casting director will usually take a picture (or digital photo nowadays) of your child and affix it to a sheet with all of your child's details on it. After seeing these pictures, many parents are horrified at the results. By taking a snapshot against a white wall right before you leave for the audition, you can offer it to the casting director to replace an inferior one. He may not accept it, but at least you tried.

For most commercial auditions, there will not be a script or lines provided to you beforehand. However, theatrical and television auditions will sometimes provide these script pages, called *sides*, to you a few days before the audition to help your child get a feel for the part and what the casting director is looking for. It is not necessary to completely memorize the sides, but it helps. The most important thing is that you and your child make a solid choice about how to do the sides at the audition. Not knowing how to play the sides is one of the things that worries people the most. Your child can always change the way she reads the sides at the audition if the casting director asks her to try it a different way.

THE AUDITION

Be sure to arrive at the audition location plenty of time in advance but not overly early. A good five to ten minutes early is plenty of time. If you parked in a paid parking meter area, be sure you brought along enough quarters to plug them throughout the audition time and also take note whether the meters are one- or two-hour meters. It is recommended you bring only yourself and your child to an audition, but if you have another young child who must accompany you, it would be a good idea to park in a flat-fee or hourly parking area so you do not have to go feed the meter every hour.

When you enter the front office, you will see a secretary who will have a sign-in sheet. You will need to write down your child's name, your agent and her phone number, and your child's Social Security number. Do not give the secretary your child's headshot and résumé; you will do that later. After signing in, it is all about waiting for your child's time to come. When your child's name is called, he will proceed into the casting area alone. This may frighten parents the first time, and it will always be a stressful time, but it is important for the casting director to see and talk to your child alone to gauge his personality and how he delivers the material.

You can talk to your child about the audition process and let him know that you will be right outside the door in the waiting area if he needs you. It is important to let your child know what to expect when he enters the audition room with all of those strange people looking at him and a video camera catching his every move.

Once your child enters the room, he will meet the casting director and a few associates. Make sure your child knows to say hello to everyone in the room individually. Also, when asked his name, he needs to be strong and confident in even this small detail. The casting director will usually then have her assistant turn on the video camera and ask your child to sit down. They will begin by asking your child some easy questions about himself: how old he is, what grade he's in school, how long he has been acting, his favorite color, and so on. This not only helps your child relax, but also gives the casting director some additional insight that may later help her pull out various emotions from your child.

The audition will then turn to the sides that you received the previous day or even that day in the waiting room. If you child has not memorized the entire sides, he should listen to the casting director read the other lines and then read his lines from the script. The casting director may ask your child to try it a different way or maybe even try it without the script. Your child should be truthful if he has not memorized the script. When they are done with the reading, someone will usually take a picture as mentioned earlier and then thank your child and bring him back into the waiting room.

After the audition, be supportive for your child. You'll need to sign out at the front desk. This is also the time where you can try to give the secretary your child's headshot and résumé as well as the instant photo you took at home. If she refuses, saying she has all she needs, smile and thank her and set out for your next appointment or for home.

There will naturally be a tendency to want to ask your child, "How did it go?" as soon as you leave the office. It is OK to ask her, but keep in mind that the usual reply you will get is simply "OK." Reassure her and praise her for doing her best and leave it at that. If the casting director wants to see your child again, he will contact your agent for a callback—another chance for your child to wow them and get the part. The same process applies from before. Many of the parents I have worked with say it helps to wear the same clothing outfit that your child wore during the first audition because it may remind the casting director what sparked his interest in your child. Plus, he will be able to use the original photo!

This audition does have one noticeable difference, however. In addition to the casting director, there will likely be a few more people at this audition than at the previous one. This can include the producer, the director, and other people who are involved in creating the production.

Your child may also be given new sides to replace the old ones or in addition to the old ones. But essentially, this audition should be a little less stressful because you know they are interested in your child and your child is now more familiar with the role and the production.

While following up is a good practice with agents and managers, calling the casting office about a role your child has auditioned for is not recommended. Usually your agent will hear how an audition was received by the casting director only if the role is to be offered. Rarely, a casting director may let the agent know it was down to two to three performers, including your child.

13
CHAPTER
The Jobs

YOU'VE MADE IT THROUGH THE AUDITION PROCESS AND subsequent callbacks and finally, you get the call you have been waiting for from your agent—your child booked a part! Your agent will let you know the date, location, and call time for your child's scene(s) and may ask you to come into his office to sign the employment contract. If your agent doesn't have the contract, you will receive it when you arrive at the set. Under no circumstances should your child begin working before you sign the contract! If there are any problems or questions with the contract, or if it differs in any way from your previous under-standing of your child's terms of employment, then contact your agent immediately. Again, under no circumstances should your child work at all until you have signed a contract.

Be sure to get on the Internet and print out detailed turn-by-turn direc-tions to the set as soon as you can. If you have the time, it is helpful to actually drive the route from your house to the stage or location at around the same time as your call time. You may be surprised how dif-ferent the streets look in the wee hours of the morning! By driving to the set a day or so before you are scheduled, you can also get an idea of where you will park. Keep an eye out for signs such as "Extras Parking in Rear" (that is, parking for background performers) and "Principals Only."

A day on a set is different for television, film, and commercial pro-ductions. In fact, not only do they differ from each other, but not every film set will be the same as the next. What follows in this chapter is more of a combination of what you can expect on both a film and a television production set.

WHAT TO BRING

The night before the job, gather up everything you will need the next day. To start working on the set, you will need to present your child's Social Security card (or number), your child's SAG card if he has one, a work permit, and filled-out I-9 employment form. You should also bring a passport or original birth certificate. Another good idea is to get a minor identification card from the Department of Motor Vehicles. These usually cost only five dollars and are invaluable for use as an identification card for employment, boarding an airplane, and so on. You should also pack a day bag of essential items such as a towel, bathrobe, tissues, snacks, books (for both of you), crafts, puzzles, medication, sunblock, raincoat, sweatshirt, toys, and other things you may need during the day. Portable folding chairs are very popular on the set as well. Also, don't forget that if your child will be schooled on the set, you are responsible for bringing assignments and books to the set.

It is also important to stress the things that you should *not* bring. Provisions are made on the set for the minor actor and one parent or guardian. While it is tempting to bring along another sibling, spouse, grandparent, or friend, especially when it's a project with a well-known actor, explain to them that you cannot bring them along. If you are single and have other children to care for, you need to either find a caregiver for your additional children or designate a guardian for your working child to look after her welfare on the set. The guardian must be over the age of eighteen and have written permission to act as a guardian while on the set.

Video and still cameras should also be left at home. As a parent, you will no doubt want to have mementos of your child's first day on the set, but a camera is discouraged. Instead, you can use your call sheet, script, and other handouts as a reminder of the day. If you absolutely, positively must bring a camera to the set, take photos only with the permission of the director or AD. If you have permission to take pictures, always announce "Flashing!" loudly before you click the shutter to let others know you are taking pictures. Pictures are usually only allowed after a scene is finished and the production is moving to the next set.

A TYPICAL SET

It is important to note early on in this chapter that every set is different. Sometimes you will be on a big studio lot such as Warner Bros., Disney, or Universal, and other times it will be a plain-looking warehouse ten miles away in Panorama City. Rather than walking you through both scenarios individually, I follow with a generalization combining the two environments. Both types of locations share common procedures.

You should plan on arriving at the location fifteen to twenty minutes before your call time. When you get there, you will see several signs along with someone directing traffic out in front. There are usually "Extras Park in Rear" signs and other variations for other cast and crew. Go ahead and ask the attendant where to park and state whether your child is a guest star, lead, featured, and so on. Include your child's name and the part he is playing. Chances are the attendant will have you on his list and will direct you to parking that is at least a little closer than the spaces where you see the line of extras parking.

Once you manage to find a parking spot, go ahead and enter the lot or production area. Sometimes you will receive instructions on who to see when you arrive, but if you do not, ask someone where the wardrobe check-in is located and make your way there. If you have a specific wardrobe that the set is providing, the wardrobe crew will sign it out to you. This may also include accessories such as glasses, hats, backpacks, or buttons. If you were told to bring your own wardrobe, you are also eligible for a wardrobe fee. This fee is variable based on the number of changes of clothes you provide, so it is best to ask the AD about the wardrobe reimbursement. Once you receive your wardrobe, you will be told where the dressing room and/or your trailer is so your child can change.

SAG rules require that productions provide cast members under the age of eighteen a separate dressing area from those used for adults and that no minor can share a dressing room with another minor of the opposite sex. The AD will probably give you a one-line schedule and a shooting schedule, which is the tentative plan for the day. On these schedules are scene numbers, page numbers, cast names, character names, and set locations. It is important to remember that this schedule is only a plan for the day and it does usually change.

The AD will then get you started and give you a time to be in makeup and may come and knock on your door when he is ready for you. Before you go into makeup, be sure your child is in her wardrobe, than get checked out one final time by the wardrobe department to make sure everything fits. After you get the OK by wardrobe, head over to makeup. Even if your child has perfect skin, she will still need varying degrees of makeup to look normal under studio lights. If the scenes she is shooting are outdoors in bright sunlight, it is a good idea to apply sunblock to your child's face early in the morning so that it is dry before she has makeup applied. After a final check, makeup will either send you back to your dressing room or off to the set.

If you still have time and are directed toward your dressing room, now is another good time to go over the lines with your child. If it is his first role, he is going to be extremely nervous. Reassure your child that everything is going to be OK, and it is supposed to be fun. Someone will knock on your door or your child's name will be heard over a loudspeaker announcing his call to the set. Pick up your collapsible chair and your book and lead your child out to his big scene.

The set is a hive of activity with people running all over trying to get it looking perfect for the next scene. Report to the AD and he will show you and your child where to go. At this point, fight the urge to stay by your child's side and take a seat someplace off-set but still within site of your child. California law is very specific about how the director handles parents on the set. Do not, under any circumstances, allow the director to place you out of sight and sound of your child.

The subject of remaining within sight and sound of your child can be a touchy one on the set, and one that both you and the set tutor should be consistently reminded of. There have been instances in which parents were not within sight and sound of their children and this led to problems, the most noted being an incident that occurred recently on the set of *Apt Pupil*. According to the lawsuit filed by several underage performers and their parents, several teenage boys were asked to remove their dancing belts, small thonglike, flesh-colored underwear used to imply nudity. The situation was complicated as many of the parents were allegedly told that to save the kids from embarrassment, the parents would have to wait in another area of the set. Some of the youngsters and their parents felt that they were taken advantage of and filmed inappropriately, so they filed lawsuits, which led to a barrage of name-calling between the lawyers for the prosecution and those of the production company. The lawsuit was later dropped; however, the lesson of being within sight and sound of your child at all times remains.

The director will go over blocking with your child and the other actors and may even do a rehearsal.

Finally, the second AD will announce, "Background to one please!" and the background actors, will take their starting positions and wait for their next cue. The first AD or the director will then ask the lead actors to take their positions and the camera operators will make some final adjustments. When the moment arrives to start shooting, it will go something like this:

"All right, on a bell please!"

[Sound of one bell.]

"Camera rolling!"

"Speed!"

[Clapboard.]

"Background action!"

"Action!"

(If you have any questions about any of these terms, please refer to the glossary.)

After the scene is done or at the director's discretion, he will usually yell "Cut!" and this will be followed by the sound of two bells and the second AD asking the background actors to go back to one. Sometimes the director will check playback in the monitor before announcing he wants to "print" or to redo the scene again. When everything is done on that particular set, the director will say, "Moving on," which means the camera and lights and other personnel are clear to start setting up at their new location.

If this was your child's only scene, head back to the dressing room, have her change back into the clothes she came in, and return the wardrobe neatly to the wardrobe department. You will also need to sign out of the lot when you leave. Congratulations! You and your child have survived her first job!

Schooling

If your child has multiple scenes or happens to get a series regular or lead role, there are certain other requirements you will have during the day. If your child spends considerable time on the set (this is arbitrary but usually equals five hours), then the producer is required to schedule sufficient time during the day for schooling. If your child works the entire day, then a minimum of three hours of schooling should be allowed, with schooling periods of at least twenty minutes each. The schooling area should provide for uninterrupted instruction. This means it should be away from the actual production area in quiet surroundings.

If this is the first time your child will be missing school because of work, you should have already checked with the school regarding its policy on excused and unexcused absences. Talk to your child's teacher and arrange how assignments will be collected and handed back in. If there is a test scheduled, find out when it can be rescheduled or if the on-set tutor can administer the exam. You should also ask if there are any duplicate textbooks and materials that can be used by the tutor. It is up to the parent to make sure that the school's academic standards are adhered to on the set and that his or her child does not fall behind.

Another important consideration is whether or not physical education is required by the school during the time your child is absent. If the set provides a tutor, it must also provide a safe play area for your child and other children to have fun in. This can include a basketball half-court or an area to run around in. These playtimes may or may not meet the physical education requirements for your child's school. Check with the principal on the exact requirements for PE and if it will be necessary to schedule makeup PE classes. Please stress to your child that the set is *not* playtime. Running around on the set is a big *no* due to the amount of cables and expensive equipment. Restrict running and horsing around to the play area.

The studio teacher assigned to a production has to meet certain guidelines to be approved by the state as a studio teacher. These include being certified in both elementary and secondary teaching credentials in the state of California as well as passing a written exam upon applying for or renewing her credentials. The production must provide a studio teacher on the set for children under sixteen years old and one teacher must be provided for every group of ten minors on a production.

The studio teacher also has a responsibility for your child's welfare. The studio teacher supervises the health and safety of children under sixteen and keeps an eye on working conditions, surroundings, signs of fatigue, and strenuous activity that affects their strength and stamina. It is also up to the teacher to stress and enforce the child labor guidelines. The total number of hours a child can work on a set is determined by his age: under six—six hours; six to eight years—eight hours; nine to fifteen years—nine hours; sixteen to seventeen years—ten hours. It is important to make sure that your studio teacher is performing her duty in looking out for your child's welfare. If you believe the teacher's interests are vested with the production company and not your child, contact your union or agent immediately. If you think your child is being overworked, let the studio teacher know and she will talk to the director or AD. This lets you off the hook and lets the studio teacher be "the bad guy." Always be sure to thank a studio teacher for looking after your child's interests if she does a good job. It is very demanding work.

If you are working the majority of the day, lunch will be served in a common area around 1 or 2 P.M. Also in this area will be a table called the craft services table with lots of goodies such as fruits, vegetables, candy, drinks, and assorted snacks. There may even be one table for both production cast and crew and a separate one for extras. Resist the temptation to treat it as a buffet and take half of the table back with you. Be courteous and take only what you can eat; don't stock up for the winter! I've seen people swipe the entire box of little fish crackers and while they were walking away, the whispers and bad looks from other cast members continued even when they turned the corner.

Commercial Sets

There are some ways in which a commercial set differs from the traditional television and film set that has been discussed previously. A commercial production can be shot in one day or may take two to three days depending on the complexity. You may think that two days is a long time to shoot a thirty-second commercial, but it's critical to get the right message through to the consumer, and that takes time. Every little detail must be perfect and signed off by the advertising company as well as the client.

A good movie to rent that humorously portrays the making of a commercial is *Life with Mikey*, with Michael J. Fox and Nathan Lane. While some of the details are highly exaggerated in the film, it does show how rigorous shooting a simple commercial can be. In the case of a commercial for food, such as cereal or ice cream, your child will be expected to taste the product and smile as if he likes it—whether he does or not. There is usually a bucket provided off-camera to spit out the product between takes so your child does not have to swallow the product after every take. There are some products that simply do not look right on camera, so they may be substituted with other things. Ice cream is incredibly hard to deal with under the hot studio lights. Milk also does not look white under studio lights, so another white liquid may be substituted for close-ups.

A commercial production varies depending on the product, such as food, clothes, video games, or school supplies. One thing they all have in common is the numerous takes to get exactly what the director is looking for. The director may ask your child to do several takes, each time emphasizing a different word. Doing the same thing over and over may be stressful for your child, so if you can tell she is getting flustered and is ready to explode, ask if you can take a few minutes to calm your child down and talk to her. As in every production, time is money, but most directors would rather take ten minutes to let your child calm down than waste the next half hour with bad takes.

14

CHAPTER

Money

IT IS A SAD FACT THAT MOST OF THE PUBLICITY SURROUNDING young performers in the industry revolves around the subject of money. What most people do not realize is that those actors getting all the screen time and suing their parents over millions of dollars are just a small percentage of those who actually make money. The majority of performers young and old do not make millions of dollars in profit; rather, they barely get by or live a modest living.

For instance, the standard rate for a principal actor on a one-hour taped show is $776 for a one-hour day (source: *www.aftra.org*). Assuming your child was hired just for the day, that would mean your pay voucher would equal roughly $800 for that particular amount of work. Minors are not immune to paying taxes on their earnings, so right away there is approximately $380 taken out of that balance. Next, subtract the 15 percent that will go to your manager and the 10 percent that will go to your agent. An additional 15 percent by law must be deposited into your child's Coogan trust account. Your SAG dues are calculated based on your earnings, so you can figure on about $40 going to your union.

This leaves your child with $60 profit from a day's worth of work. With this $60 you must also pay for part of your child's lessons, gas to and from the shooting location and auditions, headshot shooting and duplication, as well as maybe a cheeseburger on the way home. Is it any wonder that former child stars try to pound into people's heads that it is not about the money?

The United States is rather unique in its belief that a child's earnings belong to the child and not the parent. The battle over the money a child performer earns has been fought for decades and continues to be a source of frustration for young performers rights organizations. Even though we have come a long way, there are still parents who assume that their child's earnings belong to them and so they spend the money wildly and without thought. One severe example is when a popular child actor's father purchased a multimillion-dollar private jet, saying that his son needed it to fly to auditions since they lived a couple of hours away from Los Angeles.

Because of the growing number of lawsuits involving former child actors suing their parents for money that was never saved for them, an old law called the Coogan Law has been revised and amended to provide more realistic expectations of production companies and parents of performers.

THE COOGAN LAW

The Coogan Law is named for former actor Jackie Coogan, who was thrust into the limelight at a mere seven years old when he appeared in the Charlie Chaplin film *The Kid*. Jackie was then signed by Metro Pictures into a lucrative $2 million contract with a $500,000 signing bonus. This was an enormous sum of money in the 1920s and is still not bad today! When Jackie's father passed away, he went to his mother and asked for the money that had been saved. He was told there was nothing left, and after a court battle, he was left with barely $100,000 of the millions he had earned as a child.

As a result of Jackie's story, California introduced the Coogan Law, which has since been rewritten many times. It has managed to stabilize now and is officially called Senate Bill 1162, or just SB 1162, and was signed into law by former California governor Gray Davis. Under the new Coogan Law, the earnings are the separate and distinct property of the child rather than the community property of the parents. In addition, the law covers 100 percent of all minors' contracts and sets aside 15 percent of the gross earnings into a separate trust account, leaving the remaining 85 percent to cover the operating expenses of the child's career. This is not to say that only 15 percent can be set aside; the child and the parent can petition the court to allow more than that figure to be set aside on a case-by-case basis.

It is not the responsibility of the parent to make deposits into the account; it is that of the production company. The trust will appoint a trustee who will need to file a series of papers within ten days of the signing of the contract that includes account numbers, a statement, the name of the child, and the name of the trustee so that the funds can be deposited by the company in a timely matter. All of these documents must be sworn to by the trustee under penalty of perjury. After the contract and the trustee's documents are provided to the court, the production company must deposit the funds within fifteen days of receiving the court order to do so.

A great resource in setting up a trust account is the Screen Actors Guild Young Performers Committee. You can find out more about the committee in Chapter 16. Choosing an institution to handle your child's trust fund is a big one. One young performer I knew was unable to withdraw his funds for college when he turned eighteen because the local bank that was handling the trust fund did not have a specified age when it was supposed to be turned over to the child. Because there was no age on the initial contract, the bank manager refused to allow the child to withdraw the funds. What puzzled the parents was that the manager would not give them an age when the performer *would* be able to get to the funds. Make sure that the trust fund you set up is with an institution that is experienced in entertainment trust funds; it will save you a lot of hardships later on.

TAXES

Children are not exempt from paying taxes, and in fact a great number of child actors every year are audited by the Internal Revenue Service. In addition, there is society's view that any parent using money his child has earned is suspect. While there have been instances in which parents took more than they should have, it is important that you and your child understand where the money she earns goes and how it relates to her career and future.

Many parents start a company under their child's name to which their child's remaining earnings are deposited and from which money is drawn to cover career-related expenses. This is a great advantage when it comes to itemizing and determining taxes. This concept is used by thousands of working actors and actresses in the industry. By setting up a business and running your child's career like a business, you will not only help ensure that taxes are paid and adjusted accordingly but also help him know that his money is being spent and reinvested in his career so he will not feel taken advantage of in later years.

Many parents feel guilty when using their child's money to buy things like clothes, pay the rent, buy food, pay for training, and so on. This feeling is normal; however, your child should in fact be paying for expenses incurred as a result of her being a performer out of her own pocket. The fees for headshots, duplication, gas to and from auditions, snacks on the way, a new shirt just for auditions, and so on are justifiable business expenses and there is no reason a parent should be paying for it out of his own pocket. The key is to totally separate professional career items from standard living expenses. Obviously this presents problems when dealing with a single parent who may be relying almost exclusively on her child to pay the rent and all expenses.

A good filing system will help you just as much with your child's career as it does with your home expenses. You should retain and organize all receipts you pay for out of your child's earnings. This includes headshots (photography and duplication), wardrobe, entertainment (picking up the tab at a business meeting), communications (cell phone, answering service, and pager), and in some cases rent and utilities. Receipts are usually best kept organized by stapling them onto standard letter-size paper and clearly labeling what they are for.

RESIDUALS

Residuals are additional income that is generated by a repeat showing on television. Depending on the contract your child has with a particular production, residuals may or may not be offered. Generally, residuals are not offered to background actors and are mainly found in the contracts of the major performers on a show. Residuals are tracked by the Screen Actors Guild based on data provided by the production companies. The Screen Actors Guild currently has a feature that allows a performer to view and check his residuals online by simply logging into his account on the SAG website.

15
CHAPTER
Publicity

IF YOUR CHILD IS LUCKY ENOUGH TO BE WORKING regularly in television and films, at some point you will need to consider looking into ways to keep your child in the minds of both casting directors and the general public. Creating publicity does not just happen overnight, but it is something that can be achieved with a thorough plan.

When most parents think of publicity, they usually think of young heartthrobs giving the thumbs-up sign at a red carpet premiere in Westwood or at the Mann Chinese Theatre. While this type of high-profile event does yield publicity value, there are other longtime publicity avenues that are perfect for young performers and their parents to participate in together.

If your child has a leading role in either a feature film or a network television series, the publicity machine at the movie studio or network will usually provide an ample supply of publicity events throughout the run of the film or series. For a motion picture, these will include the premiere of the film of course, but will also consist of satellite interviews with television stations around the country as well as travel and appearances on national morning shows such as *Good Morning America*, *The Today Show*, and others.

Publicity for television shows is oftentimes similar to that for motion pictures. Most television networks kick off their fall programming schedules with a press day when they invite television stations, radio stations, and other publicity outlets to their production company offices so that reporters can interview all of the actors for their network in one place and at one time. The stations are assigned an office and the stars rotate through all the offices, giving short interviews and sound clips at each stop.

MOVIE PREMIERES

Getting invited to a movie premiere is a mixture of luck, persistence, and networking. Unless your child is near the top of the food chain among young performers, chances are that movie premieres will be out of reach. The youngsters you see at movie premieres usually have a publicity machine running behind the scenes that gets them into the premieres.

Film studios have a position in their own publicity department called the talent relations department that is dedicated to dealing with the needs of and requests from their celebrities. This department will arrange both the premieres and the transportation for the performers if they can get them into a premiere. Movie premiere tickets tend to be given out to performers who also appear on the company's film, television, or music labels. For instance, the majority of invitations to a premiere for a Warner Bros. film will be sent out to other Warner Bros. actors and actresses with films coming out soon or to actors who appear on Warner Bros. television shows.

The public sees premieres as a red-carpet event but it does not see what happens afterward. If your child is lucky enough to get invited to a premiere, be prepared for a long day or night, as the premiere experience does not stop when the film is over. If your child is invited to a premiere, it will include one guest. Additional tickets are hard, if not impossible to get. Have your manager try to negotiate for an extra ticket, but do not expect one. Once inside the theatre, guests are seated for what seems like an eternity and then either the film's executive producer or the director approaches a microphone at the front of the theatre and gives a short speech thanking everybody for coming and everybody involved in the film. Next, the lights dim and the film begins. Once the film is over, there are usually one or more parties planned at a separate location. If you are invited to attend a premiere, it is a good idea to ask if that includes the after party or if it is for the premiere only.

Movies for children have been increasing in popularity lately as studios have finally realized that a kids movie that plays during an otherwise full bill of adult films will do very well. The success of the Spy Kids and Harry Potter movies is a great example. At a movie premiere for a children's film, there is usually a party on the back lot of whatever movie studio is hosting the premiere. A favorite among this type of premieres is a screening at Universal's Cineplex Odeon theatres and then a party on a secluded part of the back lot or City Walk. Since it is a kids movie, there are games and other fun events afterward to keep kids entertained and having fun all day.

Fortunately for young performers, studios want a lot of young actors and actresses to attend their premieres for children's films, so it is easier to get invited to these types of events. In addition, many of the premieres of this type are also used as charity events for many of the children's hospitals and other youth programs in the Los Angeles area. Charity events provide another way for young performers to not only obtain publicity but also make a difference.

CHARITY EVENTS

Charity events provide many different functions for the young performer. First, they provide a safe avenue for getting one's face out there in the public. Second, they provide a way for young performers to interact with other young performers, and adults, away from the professional setting of the film or television studio. Last, and my favorite of all, it affords the young performer an opportunity to give back to the community and show her compassion for others. I have been to hundreds of events with young performers and each one was a satisfying one, rain or shine.

In Chapter 16, there is a short listing of suggested charities that I have compiled. While this is a good list, there are many ways to volunteer in your community no matter where you are. These events are strictly volunteer, so do not expect some kind of appearance fee or limousine transportation to the venue. Chances are the only things you will receive are some free publicity, an event T-shirt, a brown-bag lunch, and the feeling of satisfaction that comes from doing something for the greater good.

VIDEO GAME LAUNCHES

The video game unveiling is becoming more and more popular. As your child certainly knows, video games are immensely popular and some are even more profitable than a feature film. Realizing that celebrity sells, manufacturers of video games have begun throwing elaborate parties to celebrate the launch of their products. These parties include a barrage of mainstream press and specialty magazine editors but also young performers and celebrities whom the makers want to have seen playing their games.

These events are usually booked by professional publicists through the video game companies, but if your child is reasonably well known, it is possible to submit his name to their publicity departments directly.

TEEN MAGAZINES

Teen magazines have been around for years and chances are, you too remember the days of reading about your favorite young celebrities and tearing out the pinups and splattering them around your room. Teen magazines are still a staple when it comes to mass media publicity; however, in recent years their features have been limited mainly to a specific genre of entertainment: music.

The focus of teen magazines follows a cycle that rotates between actors and musicians. The early and mid-nineties focused on actors and actresses. Popular subjects for pinups and articles at that time were Kirk Cameron, Eddie Furlong, Leonardo DiCaprio, Jonathan Taylor Thomas, Devon Sawa, Jodie Sweetin, and Candace Cameron. With the rise in popularity of Hanson in 1996, slowly but surely the focus switched from actors and actresses to musicians. Gone was Jonathan Taylor Thomas and in were Hanson, the Backstreet Boys, and *NSYNC. The music cycle continued in full force, adding such teen idols as Aaron Carter, Billy Gilman, Stevie Brock, and DreamStreet.

We are currently seeing another shift in the teen magazine market back to the actor and actress mode. With the popularity of boy bands waning, a new breed of young performers is emerging, shifting the magazines back toward the young actor and actress. This shift can be seen in the popularity of Hilary Duff, from the Disney Channel's *Lizzie Maguire*, who also has released several CDs and even had a television special that covered her birthday party in Hawaii. On the guys side, singer and actor Jesse McCartney is doing well after breaking off from the boy band DreamStreet.

With young actors and actresses becoming more popular for the magazines, the publications are opening up their "up and coming" sections more and more to the new crop of young performers in the business. This provides new young performers a great chance of being featured in "the rags" and who knows, maybe your child will be a favorite and a magazine will ask to do a feature article on her someday.

Submitting to the teen magazines is a fairly simple process and does not require a professional publicist, although it helps. You can find a list of teen magazines and their editors in Appendix 4. Submitting to the editors is a lot like submitting to agents and casting directors: simply send a black-and-white photo of your child and a short biography. If they are interested they will either rewrite the bio that you sent in or contact your child for an additional interview.

WEBSITES

Of all the publicity opportunities for young actors that I discuss here, the easiest and most immediate way to gather publicity is through a website for your child. For many parents, the thought of putting personal information and photographs on the Internet is a frightening one, but it does not have to be. By using your common sense and doing it the right way, you can create not only a professional appearance for your child on the Internet but a safe one as well.

There is no shortage of companies on the Internet that will build you a website either for free or for a small fee. In fact, if your child becomes popular enough, chances are you will have several offers to create a website come in simultaneously through your agent or manager. Most of these offers are from fans who want to promote your child, but a word of caution surrounding random submissions from fans is needed. There are predators out there that have their own best interests in mind and not yours or your child's.

So what do you do if you need a website? You can ask friends or family if they know how to build a website or know somebody who does. Or, you can do it yourself if you know how. A third option is to go with a company that is known for creating entertainment websites for celebrities.

Most kids these days will have their first experience with creating websites by the time they are in sixth grade. The introduction of new media classes in elementary and high school curricula has ushered in a tremendous amount of young students who can build a website. You need to be careful, however, if you think that your young nephew would be the perfect person to design and maintain a website for your child. While your niece or nephew might have the basic skills for designing a website, whatever you put out there on the Web will be your child's calling card and will possibly be seen by millions of Internet users. The number one consideration for a website has to be an aesthetic one. If it is full of flashy buttons and bright colors and looks like a thirteen-year-old designed it, politely say thank you but you are going to look at a few more designs. It can be tough telling a relative no, but again, this is your child's professional home.

I started out in the business of creating websites for a variety of young performers and have amassed quite a list of performers that I have been privileged to be associated with. They include Mason Gamble, Wil Horneff, the Moffatts, Joseph Ashton, Mathew Valencia, Erica Mer, and Kevin Zegers. Over the course of almost ten years, I have seen many celebrity webpage companies come and go, including a service with a huge budget and a client list that boasted Jonathan Taylor Thomas, Candace Cameron, David Hasselhoff, and other big stars. The truth of the matter is that there is very little money to be had for these companies. Internet advertising is just starting to be profitable, and most of what little money they do make still comes directly from your pocketbook.

There is also a growing number of individuals who provide free fan sites for entertainment clients and seem to feed off the status they get from representing a good number of performers. In the publicity business, as with most businesses, you get what you pay for. If somebody offers to design and host a website for your child free of charge, you really need to question the motives of such an individual or entity. What will that person get out of promoting your child for free? Usually the answer is that these individuals crave some kind of connection to the inside world of the child performer. They want and need to be able to say, "Yeah, I know X," to their friends. If somebody offers to do your website for free, I suggest running the other way.

Whether you design your own website or have somebody else do it, a professional website should incorporate standard elements. First, as soon as you can, register your child's name as a domain name or Internet address. You can do this at a domain name registration website or by calling a local Internet provider. The person who registers your domain name does not have to be the one who designs or hosts your site. By registering the name right away, you prevent people known as squatters from registering it out from under you and then charging you big bucks to give you control over the name. The website should include a printable résumé on a white background and also a small photo gallery where you can put up screen captures from your child's projects or part of his modeling portfolio. Many websites also incorporate community elements such as message boards and chat rooms. You should be wary of these interactive elements, as there are laws governing obtaining personal information from children under thirteen. You should make sure the professional photographs you post on your child's website are "for hire" to avoid any copyright complaints from the photographer. Studios are very lenient about letting actors post pictures or a small clip from a show on their website. Just don't post the whole show.

Finally, it may seem that having more than one official or sanctioned website means your child is more popular, but all it does is water down the popularity of your official website. Oftentimes having more than one website means that any one of them can put up information that may or may not be true or accurate. Also, the feeling of competition may be frustrating and cause bitter feelings among the people you have sanctioned as official or licensed. Keep it simple: One official website. Period. Unfortunately, there is usually not anything you can do about unofficial fan sites.

FAN MAIL

Once your child has had one or two television appearances or a motion picture role, she will begin to receive fan mail via her agent. You may be startled at first, wondering how the fans found out your child's information. The Screen Actors Guild maintains an actor locator service that is used primarily by casting directors to locate the representative of a particular performer. The service has also been known to be used by professional autograph seekers.

When you receive your child's first piece of fan mail it is OK to be excited. Usually the letter will ask your child a little more about himself, and near the bottom it will say something like "One more thing: it would be really great if you could send me an autographed picture of yourself—it would make my day." I recommend making up a bio sheet and a form letter for answering such requests. If you send an autographed photo, be sure to personalize it for each fan. Oftentimes the professional autograph seeker will say, "Since it is a gift, please do not personalize." This is a clue that the photo will soon be up on eBay® or sold to a dealer.

It is wise to screen all fan mail that your child receives. While most fans' requests are harmless, once in a while inappropriate and sometimes obscene requests will come in from prisons, mental institutions, and the general public. One young actor I know routinely receives requests for fingernail clippings and locks of hair so that the writer can clone him when the technology is available!

Finally, always use your agent's return address on the envelope, even if you are mailing from a different city. Many parents will set up a post office box for their child when they create the child's company. In that case, you can use either address. The bottom line is not to distribute any information that would let a fan locate your home address or telephone number.

STARTING A FAN CLUB

A fan club is a way to build a base of people interested in your child's career. One of the new terms for a fan club is a *street team*. While the fan clubs you remember probably consisted of receiving a photo and a cheesy membership card, fan clubs today are sophisticated and can contribute significantly to your child's success. As with a website, you may have people writing in from all over saying they would like to start an official fan club or sanctioned fan club for your child. Under no circumstances should you relinquish control over your child's name and likeness to somebody who approaches you or your child in this way.

Setting up a fan club is a lot easier if you have already done the legwork of setting up a company for your child's career. A fan club package at the very least consists of a quarterly newsletter, interviews, personal facts, photos, and of course the membership card. It may be tempting to include cute things such as stickers, engraved pens or pencils, or a bookmark; however, these expenses can add up very quickly, and you can't expect a child the same age as yours to dish out thirty to forty dollars a year for a fan club membership. Keep it simple and keep it priced low, say, in the twelve- to fifteen-dollar range. One of the most expensive fan club letters ever sent out was Elijah Wood's *Elijah's World* magazine, which was a full-color magazine. The magazine published only four issues and is now a collector's item. A full-color magazine is definitely overkill.

WHEN TO HIRE A PUBLICIST

If your child is lucky enough to be working steadily and wants to remain in the public eye, it may be time to hire a professional publicist who can assist you in the promotional aspects of your child's career. There is no exact time when a publicist is needed. In fact, many performers hire a publicist for blocks of time, then take a few months off and then start back up again. A publicist is another expense for your child, so it is a decision that needs to be considered carefully. The cost to hire a publicist varies tremendously based on the experience, client load, and reputation of the publicist.

When you hire a publicist, he will need some time to get materials in order and create press kits and other promotional materials. For this reason, most publicists will ask for a service period no shorter than three months. The publicist will create a publicity kit for your child that will include your child's headshot, a biography, a personal facts list, a résumé, and any press clippings and additional information that may be of interest.

Hiring a publicist by no means will get you into every movie premiere. However, the publicist will know of other public events and organizations that your child will be able to participate in. The publicist will also aid your manager and agent in getting your child nominated for many of the young performers award shows. If you do not already have a website for your child, the publicist may also include website design and hosting as part of her publicity package.

16

Other Resources

IN ADDITION TO THE MANY RESOURCES I HAVE MENTIONED
so far, there are many additional resources available to you and your
child to help him through the ups and downs of being a young performer. These include publications, committees, organizations, and
individuals who care about young performers and want to do their best
to see your child succeed both in the entertainment business and in life.

SCREEN ACTORS GUILD YOUNG PERFORMERS COMMITTEE

The Screen Actors Guild Young Performers Committee (SAG YPC) held
its first meeting during the *Hollywood Reporter's* YoungStar Awards in
1995. Since then, the committee has enjoyed a permanent place in the
hearts of former and current young performers. Its meetings are frequented by several celebrity speakers who introduce new families into
the world of being a young performer in Hollywood. Currently, the
YPC meets the third Tuesday of every month at the Screen Actors Guild
headquarters on Wilshire Boulevard. Attendees receive a handbook
detailing the working regulations for minors and great advice from a
variety of sources. There is no need to preregister to attend; simply
show up at 7 P.M. at the SAG office and follow the signs to the meeting
place.

A MINOR CONSIDERATION

One of the most celebrated organizations that helps young performers deal with their stardom and prevent tragedy is A Minor Consideration (AMC), founded by former child actor Paul Petersen of *The Donna Reed Show*. Founded in 1999, AMC strives to provide a comfortable atmosphere for present and former child actors and actresses to meet together and discuss their problems and victories among friends. AMC also is involved in situations when a young performer is in trouble with the law or involved in an emergency situation. AMC has been instrumental in obtaining new legislation regarding the employment of premature babies for movies and television, as well as closely monitoring the working conditions on SAG-franchised productions.

OAKWOOD TEMPORARY HOUSING

The Oakwood Temporary Housing complex is located adjacent to the Warner Bros. studios on Barham Avenue in Burbank. For many years these facilities have been the preferred location of Warner Bros. and other studios to house their young TV and film actors. As a result of this constant influx of new actors and actresses every year, the Oakwood complex maintains an active clientele of both novice and experienced young performers. Every Sunday, the Oakwood hosts a Sunday brunch for its young performers and provides seminars and classes for those staying at the residence. It is a gated community accessible only with a key card; however, you can speak to a residence associate by letting the guard know you are interested in making a reservation.

THE *HOLLYWOOD REPORTER* ANNUAL SHOWBIZ KIDS ISSUE

The *Hollywood Reporter* Annual Showbiz Kids Issue is a special edition of *The Hollywood Reporter* that features only young performers. You can pick up last year's issue at the magazine's office at 5055 Wilshire Boulevard, Suite 600, in Los Angeles. The issue is broken down into articles that include advice from casting directors and agents, short sidebars on young performers who made an impact during the past year in the "Ones to Watch" section, and advertisements that feature

---

an entire agency's or management company's clientele. You may also see that some children have their own advertisements in the issue. All of the advertisements are generally paid for by the client, that is, you. Your talent agency may ask you to chip in for the cost of its ad. In addition, you may elect to pay the two thousand dollars or so to have your child's own one-page ad. The choice is yours; however, I strongly recommend chipping in for the agency ad if you are asked. It is advertising for all of the agency's stars, so the cost should be negligible.

When the issue comes out, pick up a copy and read all the articles. You can make notes of some of the workshop teachers listed, some good words of advice from a casting director you've worked with, and so on. There is always a wealth of information in these issues; you just have to know how to find it and use it to your advantage.

YOUNG PERFORMER MAGAZINE

Young Performer is a publication created by John Kelleher that details all aspects of being a young performer in the entertainment field. Not necessarily always about television and film production, this unique industry magazine contains articles from both known and not-so-known kids. Kelleher uses the kids themselves as the journalists and most of the articles are written by young performers and only copyedited by Kelleher. There is always an article from A Minor Consideration's president, Paul Petersen, as well as an editorial column by Kelleher himself. There are feature articles on budgeting time and money as well as unique articles such as traveling the United State in a theatre troupe. The cost per year is twenty dollars and subscriptions can be ordered by sending the fee to Young Performer Magazine, PO Box 460475, Aurora, Colorado 80046-0475.

CHARITIES

One of the most satisfying events I witness when working with young performers is their willingness to help others who may not be as fortunate. L.A. is a great city in which to be involved with different charities, but there are also opportunities in your local area. The following list of charities is by no means complete, but it will give you a great starting point. Giving back to the community is a wonderful experience for everybody involved, and you should encourage your child to give a little of herself. After just one time she will love it!

Kids with a Cause

Kids with a Cause was formed by Linda Finnegan in 1999 and strives to provide help to children who suffer from poverty, hunger, sickness, lack of education, abandonment, neglect, and/or abuse. Its members include more than eighty young performers in general membership as well as a youth advisory board. The charity puts on several of its own events during the year including an Academy Awards party, as well as visits to hospitals, nursing homes, and other locations to further its causes. Adults are encouraged to volunteer their time with their children. The group can be reached at (310) 407-8616 or through email at *info@kidswithacause.org*.

Actors for Kids

Actors for Kids is a charity formed in 1999 that provides an active and safe venue for performers of all ages to give their time to help those less fortunate. Actors for Kids plans numerous events throughout the year including charity sports games and meet and greets. The organization can be reached at *info@actorsforkids.org*.

The Audrey Hepburn Children's Fund

The Audrey Hepburn Children's Fund began in 1994 and moved from New York to Los Angeles in 1999. The fund is dedicated to continuing Audrey Hepburn's efforts in helping the sick and ill-treated children of the world. Some of the programs include the Audrey Hepburn Memorial Fund at the U.S. Fund for UNICEF, dedicated to educating children in Somalia, Sudan, Eritrea, Ethiopia, and Rwanda; the first Audrey Hepburn Children's House, located at Hackensack University Medical Center, offering comprehensive treatment for physically and emotionally abused children in a child-friendly environment; the Audrey Hepburn CARES Team at Children's Hospital Los Angeles, providing the very best medical and mental health services to suspected victims of child abuse; and the All Children in School Program, a recently established ten-year joint venture with the U.S. Fund for UNICEF, aimed at bringing 120 million children worldwide back to school. If you are interested in this charity, please call (310) 393-5331.

CONCLUSION

In looking back over the many pages that precede this one, I feel a great sense of wonder and amazement that I have managed to put down all this information in a book. Along with the amazement, there is also a sense of dread that I have forgotten or overlooked something important. It is the same feeling that makes me get up in the middle of the night to make sure I turned my car's headlights off.

The world of the young performer is one of small successes and many failures. Why on earth would somebody choose this lifestyle? Because there is no choice. Young performers who want to be actors or actresses know what they want to do far earlier than when they tell their parents. It is engraved in their souls.

I have seen child actors at their best and their parents at their worst. The press is inundated with the latest former child star suing his parents over money and mismanagement of his vast fortunes. There are gossip columns filled with stories of young performers sleeping with their managers, other performers of the same sex, their studio teachers, and women or men more than fifty years their senior. While these stories may have their basis in fact, the majority of young performers remain relatively unscathed from their experience.

In fact, in some cases, they turn out for the better. For many young performers, their career is relatively short. Very few can begin a career at an early age and transition to adult roles after high school or college. Kids who participate in acting gain valuable lessons that will help them in their everyday lives whether or not they pursue a career in the industry in their adult lives. Acting teaches young children about rejection.

The audition experience for a young actor can be a tremendous advantage during her adult job hunt and interviews. Indeed, not only will she have had the experience of being turned down for a job, but the entire job interview is similar to an audition! Being able to exude confidence and an appropriate demeanor with a prospective employer can mean the difference between getting a job and getting shuffled to the next interview. Acting teaches a lot about life.

Success is a hard thing to measure. Some parents consider their child a successful young performer when he has booked one job. Others may not consider their child a success even after she has had five films and two television series. To me, each goal a child reaches is a success. Let me encourage you to look for your child's small successes as he builds his career. Encouragement from family is extremely important and can be the difference between growing up happy and healthy and growing up miserable. It is important that you verbally recognize these little successes in life: a good audition, an A on a report card, signing with an agent—anything and everything.

I believe each parent sets out with his or her child's best interests in mind. Sometimes it just gets twisted. The business of acting is compelling to say the least. Not only are those who want in victims to its siren, but also those that have had a taste. The camaraderie and pats on the back that you and your child feel from producers, directors, and fellow actors only intensify the need for that kind of attention. Many young actors who do not have a good support system at home find themselves in trouble with the law and/or seek to fill that void with drugs and alcohol.

In the foreword, Paul Petersen talked about two things: education and an exit strategy. Education is not limited to school and set tutors. Education is everywhere. From memorization of lines to tax deductions, your child will receive an education that includes so many different experiences. You and your child will make many friends and perhaps a few enemies. Never turn your back on an opportunity you have not explored. Fuel your child's curiosity and thirst for knowledge.

As Paul mentioned, and I emphasized, an exit strategy is key to either a bad or a good experience in the business. If your child simply flickers out, there will be resentment. An exit strategy that includes support and love will benefit you and your child for years to come.

Use your parental instincts wisely and remember it is your child's life and career, not yours. Being a performer is a satisfying career full of magnificent ups and some serious downs. But in the end, actors act because they have to.

If you would like to talk one-on-one with me about a career in show business for your child, please visit the web site *www.kidsinthebiz.com.*

Best wishes, and good luck.

APPENDIX 1
Talent Agencies in California

Abrams Artists Agency
9200 Sunset Blvd., Suite 1130
Los Angeles, CA 90069
(310) 859-0625

Acme Talent and Literary
    Agency
4727 Wilshire Blvd., Suite 333
Los Angeles, CA 90010
(323) 954-2263

Agency West Entertainment
5750 Wilshire Blvd., Suite 640N
Los Angeles, CA 90036
(323) 857-9050

Aimee Entertainment
15840 Ventura Blvd., Suite 215
Encino, CA 91436
(818) 783-3831

AKA Agency
6310 San Vicente Blvd.,
    Suite 200
Los Angeles, CA 90048
(323) 965-5600

Allure Model and Talent Agency
5556 Centinela Ave.
Los Angeles, CA 90066
(310) 306-1150

Alvarado Rey Agency
8455 Beverly Blvd., Suite 410
Los Angeles, CA 90048
(323) 655-7978

Amatruda, Benson, and
    Associates
91707 Wilshire Blvd., Suite 500
Beverly Hills, CA 90210
(310) 276-1851

Amsel, Eisenstadt, and Fraxier
5757 Wilshire Blvd., Suite 510
Los Angeles, CA 90036
(323) 939-1188

Angel City Talent
4741 Laurel Canyon Blvd.,
    Suite 101
Valley Village, CA 91607
(818) 760-9980

Artists Management Agency
835 Fifth Ave., Suite 411
San Diego, CA 92101
(619) 233-6655

Bobby Ball Agency
4342 Lankershim Blvd.
Universal City, CA 91602
(818) 506-8188

Baron Entertainment
5757 Wilshire Blvd., Suite 659
Los Angeles, CA 90036
(323) 936-7600

Marian Berzon Agency
336 E. 17th St.
Costa Mesa, CA 92627
(949) 631-5936

Brand Agency
1520 Brookhollow Dr., Suite 39
Santa Ana, CA 92705
(714) 850-1158

Buchwald Talent Group
6500 Wilshire Blvd.,
   Suite 2210
Los Angeles, CA 90048
(323) 852-9555

Iris Burton Agency
8916 Ashcroft Ave.
Los Angeles, CA 90048
(310) 288-0121

Chateau Billings
8489 W. Third St.
Los Angeles, CA 90048
(323) 965-5432

Circle Talent Associates
433 N. Camden Dr., Suite 400
Beverly Hills, CA 90210
(310) 285-1585

The Clark Agency
13415 Ventura Blvd., Suite 3
Sherman Oaks, CA 91423
(818) 385-0583

Colleen Cler Agency
178 S. Victory Blvd., Suite 108
Burbank, CA 91502
(818) 841-7943

CMT Talent Agency
$8344\frac{1}{2}$ W. Third St.
Los Angeles, CA 90048
(323) 658-7072

Coast to Coast
3350 Barham Blvd.
Los Angeles, CA 90068
(323) 845-9200

Commercials Unlimited
8383 Wilshire Blvd., Suite 850
Beverly Hills, CA 90211
(323) 655-0069

Cunningham Escott Dipene
10635 Santa Monica Blvd.,
   Suite 140
Los Angeles, CA 90025
(310) 475-3336

Diverse Talent Group
1875 Century Park East,
   Suite 2250
Los Angeles, CA 90067
(310) 201-6565

Epstein-Wyckoff-Corsa-Ross,
and Associates
280 S. Beverly Dr., Suite 400
Beverly Hills, CA 90212
(310) 278-7222

5 Star Talent
2312 Janet Lee Dr.
La Crescenta, CA 91214
(818) 249-4241

Gold Liedtke Associates
3500 W. Olive Ave., Suite 1400
Burbank, CA 91505
(818) 972-4300

Beverly Hecht Agency
12001 Ventura Pl., Suite 320
Studio City, CA 91604
(818) 505-1192

Hervey Grimes Talent Agency
10561 Missouri Ave., Suite 2
Los Angeles, CA 90025
(310) 475-2010

Hollander Talent Group
14011 Ventura Blvd., Suite 202
Sherman Oaks, CA 91423
(818) 382-9800

Howard Talent West
10657 Riverside Dr.
Toluca Lake, CA 91602
(818) 766-5300

Identity Talent Agency
2050 S. Bundy Dr., Suite 200
Los Angeles, CA 90025
(310) 882-6070

Innovative Artists
1505 10th St.
Santa Monica, CA 90401
(310) 656-0400

Kazarian Spencer
and Associates
11365 Ventura Blvd.,
Suite 100
Studio City, CA 91604
(818) 755-7200

Sharon Kemp Agency
447 S. Robertson Blvd.,
Suite 204
Beverly Hills, CA 90211
(310) 858-7200

L.A. Talent
7700 Sunset Blvd.
Los Angeles, CA 90036
(323) 436-7777

Jana Luker Agency
$1923\frac{1}{2}$ Westwood Blvd.,
Suite 3
Los Angeles, CA 90025
(310) 441-2822

MGA
221 E. Walnut St., Suite 130
Pasadena, CA 91101
(818) 567-1400

The Morgan Agency
7080 Hollywood Blvd.,
Suite 1009
Los Angeles, CA 90028
(323) 469-7100

Osbrink Talent Agency
4343 Lankershim Blvd.,
   Suite 100
Universal City, CA 91608
(818) 760-2488

The Savage Agency
6212 Banner Ave.
Los Angeles, CA 90038
(323) 461-8316

Starwil Talent Agency
433 N. Camden Dr., Fourth
   Floor
Beverly Hills, CA 90210
(323) 874-1239

TAG Models
4727 Wilshire Blvd., Suite 333
Los Angeles, CA 90010
(323) 602-0344

APPENDIX 2
Talent Agencies
Throughout the United States

Alabama

Alabama Talent and Model
   Management
Tuscaloosa, AL 35402
(205) 364-8700

Cathi Larsen Agency
1675 Montclair Road
Birmingham, AL 35210
(205) 951-2445

Star Quality Talent Agency
Decatur, AL 35601
(205) 353-0773

Alaska

Alaska Image Design
Mike Robinson, Owner
600 W. 41st, Suite 102
Anchorage, AK 99503
(907) 561-5739

Cupik Warrior Productions
Eben W. Olrun, Owner and CEO
P.O. Box 110662
Anchorage, AK 99511-0662
(907) 258-2454

GetReal Casting
P.O. Box 2698
Palmer, AK 99645
(907) 745-5777

Arizona

Action Talent and Modeling
2530 E. Broadway Blvd., Suite H
Tucson, AZ 85716
(520) 881-6535

Ford/Robert Black Agency
4300 N. Miller Rd., Suite 202
Scottsdale, AZ 85251
(480) 966-2537

Signature Models and Talent
  Agency (SAG-AFTRA)
2600 North 44th St., #209
Phoenix, AZ 85008
(480) 966-1102

Arkansas

Advantage Talent and
  Promotions
1602 Green Mountain Dr., #131E
Little Rock, AR 72211
(501) 765-0043

The Agency, Inc.
802 W. 8th St.
Little Rock, AR 72201
(501) 374-8903

Ferguson Modeling and Talent
1100 W. 34th St.
Little Rock, AR 72206
(501) 375-3519

Colorado

Donna Baldwin Talent
2237 W. 30th Ave.
Denver, CO 80211
(303) 561-1199

Mattas Talent Agency
1026 W. Colorado Ave.
Colorado Springs, CO 80904
(719) 577-4704

Maximum Talent, Inc.
1660 S. Albion St., Suite 1004
Denver, CO 80222
(303) 691-2344

Connecticut

Creative Christian Arts
11 Spring Hill Ave.
Norwalk, CT 06850
(203) 849-1722

Joanna Lawrence Agency
82 Patrick Rd.
Westport, CT 06880
(203) 226-7239

Florida

Alliance Talent Group, Inc.
1940 Harrison St., Suite 300
Hollywood, FL 33020
(954) 727-9500

Azuree Talent, Inc.
1115 Kentucky Ave.
Winter Park, FL 32789
(407) 629-5025

Central Florida Talent, Inc.
2601 Wells Ave., Suite 181
Fern Park, FL 32730
(407) 830-9226

Martin and Donalds Talent
  Agency, Inc.
2131 Hollywood Blvd., #308
Hollywood, FL 33020
(954) 921-2427

Georgia

Atlanta Models and Talent, Inc.
2970 Peachtree Rd. NW, Suite 660
Atlanta, GA 30305
(404) 261-9627

Genesis Models and Talent, Inc.
1465 Northside Dr., Suite 120
Atlanta, GA 30318
(404) 350-9212

The Talent Group/Hot Shot Kids
561 W. Pike St.
Lawrenceville, GA 30045
(678) 215-1500

Hawaii

Kathy Muller Talent Agency
619 Kapahulu Ave. Penthouse
Honolulu, HI 96815
(808) 737-7917

Idaho

Blanche B. Evans Agency
    International
4311 Audubon Pl.
Boise, ID 83705-3851
(208) 344-5380

Metcalf's Modeling and Talent
1851 Century Way #3
Boise, ID 83709
(208) 378-8777

Illinois

Baker and Rowley Talent
    Agency, Inc.
1327 W. Washington, Suite 5-C
Chicago, IL 60607-1914
(312) 850-4700

Geddes Agency
1633 N. Halsted St., Suite 400
Chicago, IL 60614
(312) 787-8333

Lily's Talent Agency
1301 W. Washington, Suite B
Chicago, IL 60607
(312) 601-2345

Indiana

The Act 1 Agency (AFTRA)
6100 N. Keystone Ave.
Indianapolis, IN 46220
(317) 255-3100

Artistic Enterprises
5350 E. 62nd St.
Indianapolis, IN 46220
(317) 722-1717

Iowa

Avant Modeling and Talent
10546 Justin Dr.
Urbandale, IA 50322
(515) 251-4199

Copeland Creative Talent
$4140\frac{1}{2}$ Grand Ave.
Des Moines, IA 50312
(515) 271-5970

RSVP Talent
P.O. Box 126
Ames, IA 50010

Talent/Iowa
6545 SE Bloomfield Rd.
Des Moines, IA 50320
(515) 285-8907

Kansas

Agency Models and Talent
10 E. Cambridge Circle Dr.

Kansas City, KS 66103
(913) 342-8382

Entertainment Plus Talent
  Agency
4800 Rainbow Blvd., Suite 4
Westwood, KS 66205
(913) 262-4500

Jackson Artists Corporation
7251 Lowell Dr., Suite 200
Overland Park, KS 66204
(913) 384-6688

KansasKID Productions
$1201\frac{1}{2}$ W. Douglas
Wichita, KS 67213
(316) 680-4243

Kentucky

Cosmo Model and Talent
  Agency
7410 New LaGrange Rd., #204
Louisville, KY 40222
(502) 425-8000

Heyman Talent Inc.
3308 Brotherton Rd.
Cincinnati, OH 45209
(513) 533-3113

On Time Talent
6703 Fernview Rd., Suite 101
Louisville, KY 40291
(502) 345-8280

Louisiana

Carpe Diem Model and Talent
2007 Clearview Pkwy., Suite C

Metairie, LA 70001
(504) 454-8080

Del Corral Model and Talent
130 S. Telemachus St.
New Orleans, LA 70119
(504) 486-6335

New Orleans Model and Talent
1347 Magazine St.
New Orleans, LA 70130
(504) 525-0100

Maryland

Accurate Casting and Talent
1889 Grempler Way
Edgewood, MD 21040

The Bullock Agency
5200 Baltimore Ave., Suite 102
Hyattsville, MD 20781
(301) 209-9598

Kids International Talent
  Agency
938 E. Swan Creek Rd.,
  Suite 152
Ft. Washington, MD 20744
(301) 292-6094

Massachusetts

Model Club, Inc.
115 Newbury St., Suite 203
Boston, MA 02116
(617) 247-9020

Prestige Model and Talent
  Agency
7 Hampshire St.

Methuen, MA 01844
(978) 687-3333

Michigan

Class Modeling Talent Agency
1625 Haslett Rd.
Haslett, MI 48840
(517) 339-2777

Pastiche Models and Talent
1514 Wealthy St. SE
Grand Rapids, MI 49506
(616) 451-2181

United Talent Agency
1421 Birch Chest St.
Dearborn, MI 48124
(810) 414-7177

Minnesota

JMG Model and Talent
P.O. Box 251201
St. Paul, MN 55125
(651) 734-9618

Moore Creative Castings, Inc.
1610-B W. Lake St.
Minneapolis, MN 55408
(612) 827-3823

Wehmann Agency
1128 Harmon Pl., #205
Minneapolis, MN 55403
(612) 333-6393

Mississippi

Coast to Coast Modeling
311 Darby St.

Gulfport, MS 39503
(228) 385-5150

Donna Groff Agency, Inc.
405 Shelby St.
Rosedale, MS 38769
(662) 759-9883

Upstage Talent Agency
558 Highway 51
Ridgeland, MS 39157
(601) 898-0004

Missouri

I and I Agency, LLC
1509 Westport Rd., Suite 200
Kansas City, MO 64111
(816) 410-9950

Incognito Talent Agency
509 Olive, Suite 602
St. Louis, MO 63101
(314) 588-1002

Millennium Model and Talent
    Management
511 Delaware, Loft 100
Kansas City, MO 64105
(816) 474-8383

Montana

Rocky Mountain Talent Services
342 S. 5th Ave.
Forsyth, MT 59327
(406) 356-7525

Nebraska

Subby Anzaldo Entertainment
1042 S. 27th St.

Omaha, NE 68105
(402) 346-0100

Take 1
14344 Y St.
Omaha, NE 68137
(402) 891-0730

Nevada

Lange Talent Agency
6370 W. Flamingo Rd., Suite 44
Las Vegas, NV 89103
(702) 253-1200

Donna Wauhob Agency
3135 Industrial Rd., #204
Las Vegas, NV 89109-1122
(702) 733-1017

Alan Wazler Group
3285 W. Tompkins Ave.
Las Vegas, NV 89103
(702) 792-8000

New Hampshire

A713 Production
P.O. Box 1027
Exeter, NH 03833-1027
(603) 978-3662

New England Models Group, Inc.
55 South Commercial St.
Manchester, NH 03101
(603) 624-0555

New Jersey

Veronica Goodman Agency
P.O. Box 1535
Cherry Hill, NJ 08002
(856) 795-3133

Models on the Move Model and
    Talent Agency
1200 Route 70, Barclay Towers,
    Suite 6
P.O. Box 4037
Cherry Hill, NJ 08034
(856) 667-1060

New York

Acme Talent and Literary
60 Madison Ave., 2nd Floor
New York, NY 10010
(212) 328-0387

Agency for the Performing Arts
888 Seventh Ave., 6th Floor
New York, NY 10106
(212) 582-1500

Henderson/Hogan Talent Agency
850 Seventh Ave., Suite 1003
New York, NY 10019
(212) 765-5190

Stanley Kaplan Talent
139 Fulton St., Suite 503
New York, NY 10038
(212) 385-4400

North Carolina

Talent Link, Inc.
P.O. Box 560337
Charlotte, NC 28256
(704) 333-5404

North Dakota

Limelight International
205 N. 2nd St.

Bismarck, ND 58501
(701) 258-2869

Ohio

Amazing Entertainment
5723 Broadway Ave.
Cleveland, OH 44127
(216) 441-0647

Joe Goenner Talent Agency
10019 Paragon Rd.
Dayton, OH 45458
(937) 885-2595

Oklahoma

Actors Casting and Talent
    Services
710 W. Wilshire Blvd.
Oklahoma City, OK 73116
(405) 810-9299

Future Stars Production
2604 Bird Dr.
Oklahoma City, OK 73121
(405) 427-1784

Magna Talent Agency
710-B Wilshire Creek Blvd.
Oklahoma City, OK 73116
(405) 842-2896

Oregon

Cusick's Talent Agency, Inc.
1009 NW Hoyt St., Suite 100
Portland, OR 97209
(503) 274-8555

Carol Lukens
1931 NE 157th Ave.

Portland, OR 97230
(503) 255-3785

Danny Stoltz Casting
635 NW 16th Ave.,
    Suite A
Portland, OR 97209
(503) 227-6055

Pennsylvania

The Reinhard Agency
2021 Arch St., Suite 400
Philadelphia, PA 19103
(215) 567-2008

The Talent Group
2820 Smallman St.
Pittsburgh, PA 15222
(412) 471-8011

Rhode Island

Rhode Island Casting Service
807 Broad St.
Providence, RI 02907
(401) 941-5500

South Carolina

Maxann's Casting Company
P.O. Box 4137
745-122 Saluda St.
Rock Hill, SC 29732-6137
(803) 328-3420

Tennessee

Action Modeling and Talent
500 Pickens La.
Columbia, TN 38401
(615) 381-8033

Carvel Model and Talent
  Agency
7075 Poplar Ave.
Memphis, TN 38138
(901) 754-4747

Texas

Acclaim Talent
4107 Medical Pkwy., Suite 210
Austin, TX 78756
(512) 416-9222

The Campbell Agency
3906 Lemmon Ave., Suite 200
Dallas, TX 75219
(214) 522-8991

Tomas Agency
14275 Midway Rd., Suite 200
Addison, TX 75001
(972) 687-9181

Utah

Craze Agency
3804 S. Highland Dr., Suite 5
Salt Lake City, UT 84106
(801) 680-0660

Revolutions Talent
850 S. Richards St.
Salt Lake City, UT 84101
(801) 746-5616

Vermont

Debra Lewin Productions and
  Talent
269 Pearl St.
Burlington, VT 05401
(802) 865-2234

Virginia

The Ambassador Talent Agency
P.O. Box 1027
Stanardsville, VA 22973
(804) 978-1742

Talent Link
325 E. Bayview Blvd., Suite 203
Norfolk, VA 23503
(757) 249-2232

Washington

Colleen Bell Modeling and
  Talent Agency
14205 SE 36th St., #100
Bellvue, WA 98006
(425) 649-1113

Kid Biz Talent Agency
One Bellevue Center
411 108th Ave. NE, Suite 2050
Bellevue, WA 98004
(425) 455-8800

Topo Swope Talent
1932 1st Ave., Suite 700
Seattle, WA 98101
(206) 443-2021

Wisconsin

Jennifer's Talent Unlimited, Inc.
740 North Plankinton, Suite 300
Milwaukee, WI 53203
(414) 277-9440

Dylan Scott Talent
P.O. Box 44311
Madison, WI 53744-4311
(608) 829-3739

APPENDIX 3
State Film Offices

Alabama Center for Commerce
401 Adams Ave., Suite 630
Montgomery, AL 36104
(334) 242-4195
www.telefilm-south.com

Alaska Trade and Development
P.O. Box 110804
Juneau, AK 99811
(907) 465-2012
www.alaskafilmoffice.com

Arizona Film Commission
1700 W. Washington, Suite 220
Phoenix, AZ 85007
(602) 771-1193
www.azcommerce.com/eFilm

Arkansas Film Office
1 Capitol Mall, Room 4B-505
Little Rock, AR 72201
(501) 682-7676
www.aedc.state.ar.us/film

California Film Commission
7080 Hollywood Blvd., Suite 900
Hollywood, CA 90028
(323) 860-2960
www.commerce.ca.gov

Colorado Film Commission
1624 Broadway, Suite 1700
Denver, CO 80202
(303) 620-4500
www.coloradofilm.org

Connecticut Film Office
805 Brook St., Bldg. 4
Rocky Hill, CT 06067
(800) 392-2122
www.ctfilm.com

Delaware Film Office
99 Kings Highway
Dover, DE 19901
(800) 441-8846
www.state.de.us

Florida Film Commission
The Capitol
Tallahassee, FL 32399-0001
(850) 410-4765
www.filminflorida.com

Georgia Film, Video, and
  Music Office
285 Peachtree Center Ave.,
  Suite 1000
Atlanta, GA 30303
(404) 656-3591
www.telefilm-south.com

Hawaii Film Office
250 South Hotel St., 5th Floor
Honolulu, HI 96813
(808) 586-2570
www.hawaiifilm.com

Idaho Film Bureau
700 W. State St.
Box 83720
Boise, ID 83720-0093
(208) 334-2470
www.filmidaho.org

Illinois Film Office
100 W. Randolph, 3rd Floor
Chicago, IL 60601
(312) 814-3600
www.filmillinois.state.il.us

Indiana Film Commission
One N. Capitol Ave.,
  Suite 700
Indianapolis, IN 46204-2288
(317) 232-8829
www.state.in.us/film

Iowa Film Office
200 E. Grand Ave.
Des Moines, IA 50309
(515) 242-4726
www.state.ia.us/film

Kansas City Film Office
10 Petticoat La., Suite 250
Kansas City, MO 64106-2103
(816) 221-0636
www.kansascommerce.com

Kentucky Film Commission
500 Mero St.
2200 Capital Plaza Tower
Frankfort, KY 40601
(502) 564-3456
www.kyfilmoffice.com

Louisiana Film and Television
P.O. Box 44320
Baton Rouge, LA 70804
(888) 655-0447
www.lafilm.org

Maine Film Office
59 State House Station
111 Sewall St., 3rd Floor
Augusta, ME 04333
(207) 624-7631
www.filminmaine.com

Maryland Film Office
217 E. Redwood St., 9th Floor
Baltimore, MD 21202
(410) 333-0044 (fax)
www.mdfilm.state.md.us

Massachusetts Film Bureau
198 Tremont St., PMB #135

Boston, MA 02116
(617) 523-8388
www.massfilmbureau.com

Michigan Film Office
P.O. Box 30739
Lansing, MI 48909
(800) 477-3456
www.michigan.gov

Minnesota Film and
   TV Board
401 N. Third St., Suite 460
Minneapolis, MN 55401
(612) 332-6493
www.mnfilm.org

Mississippi Film Office
Woolfolk State Office Building
501 North West St., 5th Floor
Jackson, MS 39201
P.O. Box 849
Jackson, MS 39205
(601) 359-3297
www.visitmississippi.org/film

Missouri Film Commission
301 W. High, Room 720
P.O. Box 118
Jefferson City, MO 65102
(573) 751-9050
*www.ded.mo.gov/business/
   filmcommission*

Montana Film Office
301 S. Park Ave.
Helena, MT 59620
(406) 841-2876
www.montanafilm.com

Nebraska Film Office
P.O. Box 98907
Lincoln, NE 68509-8907
(402) 471-3680
www.filmnebraska.org

Nevada Film Office
555 E. Washington Ave.,
   Suite 5400
Las Vegas, NV 89101
(702) 486-2711
www.nevadafilm.com

New Hampshire Film Office
172 Pembroke Road
P.O. Box 1856
Concord, NH 03302
(603) 271-2665
www.filmnh.org

New Jersey Motion Picture &
   Television Commission
153 Halsey St. 5th Floor
P.O. Box 47023
Newark, NJ 07101
(973) 648-6279
www.njfilm.org

New Mexico Film Commission
P.O. Box 20003
Santa Fe, NM 87504-5003
(800) 545-9871
www.edd.state.nm.us/FILM

New York Film Office
540 Madison Ave., 30th Floor
New York, NY 10022

North Carolina Film Office
301 North Wilmington Street

Raleigh, NC 27601
(919) 733-9900
www.ncfilm.com

North Dakota Film Commission
604 East Blvd., 2nd Floor
Bismarck, ND 58505
(701) 328-2874

Ohio Film Commission
77 South High St.,
   29th Floor
P.O. Box 1001
Columbus, OH 43216-1001
www.ohiofilm.com

Oklahoma Film Commission
15 N. Robinson, Suite 802
Oklahoma City, OK 73102
(800) 766-3456
www.oklahomafilm.org

Oregon Film Office
One World Trade Center
121 SW Salmon, Suite 1205
Portland, OR 97204
(503) 229-5832
www.oregonfilm.org

Pennsylvania Film Office
200 N. 3rd St., Suite 901
Harrisburg, PA 17101
(717) 783-3456
www.filminpa.com

Rhode Island Film Commission
150 Benefit St.
Providence, RI 02903
(401) 277-3456
www.rifilm.org

South Carolina Film Office
P.O. Box 7367
Columbia, SC 29202
(803) 737-0490
www.scfilmoffice.com

South Dakota Film Commission
711 E. Wells Ave.
Pierre, SD 57501-3369
(605) 773-3301
(800) 952-3625
www.travelsd.com

Tennessee Film Office
320 6th Ave. North, 7th Floor
Nashville, TN 37243-0790
(615) 741-3456

Texas Film Commission
P.O. Box 13246
Austin, TX 78711
(512) 463-9200
www.governor.state.tx.us/film

Utah Film Commission
324 South State, Suite 500
Salt Lake City, UT 84114
(801) 538-8740

Vermont Arts Council
134 State St.
Montpelier, VT 05602
(802) 828-3384
www.vermontartscouncil.org

Virginia Film Office
901 E. Byrd St.
Richmond, VA 23219-4048
(804) 371-8204
www.film.virginia.org

Washington State Film Office
2001 Sixth Ave., Suite 2600
Seattle, WA 98121
(206) 256-6151
www.oted.wa.gov/ed/filmoffice

West Virginia Film Office
c/o West Virginia Division
    of Tourism
90 MacCorkle Ave. SW
South Charleston, WV 25303
(304) 558-2200
www.wvdo.org/tourism/film.html

Wisconsin Film Office
201 W. Washington Ave.,
    2nd Floor
Madison, WI 53703
(800) 345-6947
www.film.state.wi.us

Wyoming Film Office
I-25 and College Drive
Cheyenne, WY 82002
(307) 777-3400
www.wyomingfilm.org

APPENDIX 4
Teen Magazines

Louise A. Barile, Editor
Teen Machine
Sterling/McFadden
233 Park Ave. South
New York, NY 10003

Mary Anne Cassata, Editor
Teen Dream
Faces Publications, Inc.
210 Route 4 East, Suite 401
Paramus, NJ 07652

Leesa Coble, Editor in chief
Bop Magazine
Laufer Publishing
6430 Sunset Blvd., Suite 7a
Hollywood, CA 90088

Matt Rossman, Editor
Teen Beat
Sterling/McFadden
233 Park Ave. South
New York, NY 10003

Ellen Jurcsak, Editor
16 Magazine
Sterling/McFadden
233 Park Ave. South
New York, NY 10003

Louise A. Barile, Editor
Tiger Beat Magazine
Sterling/McFadden
233 Park Ave. South
New York, NY 10003

Christina Ferrari, Editor
Teen People
Time, Inc.
Time and Life Building
Rockefeller Center
New York, NY 10020-1393

Hedy End, Editor
Superteen Magazine
Sterling/McFadden
233 Park Ave. South
New York, NY 10003

Kelly Bryant, Senior Editor
POPSTAR!
Leisure Publishing, LLC
7598 West Sand Lake Road
Orlando, FL 32819

Brian Spero, Editor in chief
BLAST
Multi-Media International
1359 Broadway, Suite 1203
New York, NY 10018

APPENDIX 5
Other Important Addresses

Movie Studios

Columbia Pictures
10202 W. Washington Blvd.
Culver City, CA 90232-3195

Dreamworks SKG
1000 Flower St.
Glendale, CA 91201

Paramount Pictures
5555 Melrose Ave.
Los Angeles, CA 90038

Sony Culver Studios
10202 W. Washington Blvd.
Culver City, CA 90232

Twentieth Century Fox
10201 W. Pico Blvd.
Los Angeles, CA 90035

Walt Disney Studios
500 South Buena Vista
Burbank, CA 91521

Warner Bros. Ranch
3701 Oak St.
Burbank, CA 91522

Warner Bros. Studios
4000 Warner Blvd.
Burbank, CA 91522-0001

Universal Studios
100 Universal City Plaza
Universal City, CA 91608-1085

Television Studios

ABC Network
4151 Prospect Ave.
Los Angeles, CA 90027

CBS Studio City
4024 Radford Ave.
Studio City, CA 91604

CBS Television City
7800 Beverly Blvd.
Los Angeles, CA 90035

NBC Burbank
3000 W. Alameda Ave.
Burbank, CA 91523

Organizations

Looking Ahead
Actors' Fund of America
5757 Wilshire Blvd., Suite 400
Los Angeles, CA 90036
(323) 933-9244

A Minor Consideration
14530 Denker Ave.
Gardena, CA 90247
(310) 523-3691 (fax)

SAG Young Performers
   Committee
5757 Wilshire Blvd.
Los Angeles, CA 90036-5810

Publications

Back Stage West
5055 Wilshire Blvd.
Los Angeles, CA 90036

The Hollywood Reporter
5055 Wilshire Blvd.,
   Suite 600
Los Angeles, CA
   90036-6103

Variety
5700 Wilshire Blvd.,
   Suite 120
Los Angeles, CA
   90036-3644

Young Performer Magazine
P.O. Box 460475
Aurora, CO 80046-0475

APPENDIX 6
Sample Contracts

SAMPLE MANAGEMENT CO., Inc.
555 Fifty-fifth St.
Los Angeles, CA 90036

SAMPLE MANAGEMENT CO., INC.—PERSONAL MANAGEMENT
CONTRACT

CONTRACT INFO

Attached is a copy of the Manager/Artist Contract. Please take your time reading through the contract thoroughly before discussing it with me or signing. Our contracts are standard for all clients of SMC and are designed to be as fair as possible for all parties concerned. Once you have had time to go over the contract and have compiled some questions (should you have any), please feel free to give me a call so that we may go over them together.

If you would like to consult an attorney before discussing the contract or your questions with us, please feel free to do so. However, I would recommend that you choose an attorney that is familiar with entertainment industries and entertainment personal management contracts. Many attorneys or individuals who are familiar with contracts, but are not familiar with contracts such as these, may offer advice that is uninformed and/or misdirected.

On the last page of this document, you will find the instructions for signing the contracts. Please follow the directions exactly when the time comes.

POWER OF ATTORNEY

By far, this is the section of the contract that throws most people for a loop. So, let me explain the need for this particular requirement:

THE SPECIAL POWER OF ATTORNEY IS A DOCUMENT THE MANAGER NEEDS TO NEGOTIATE AND AGREE ON YOUR BEHALF, AS DESCRIBED IN THE CONTRACT. THIS POWER OF ATTORNEY IS LIMITED TO WORK IN THE ENTERTAINMENT INDUSTRY AND CANNOT BE USED FOR ANY OTHER PURPOSE. IT MUST BE SIGNED BEFORE A NOTARY PUBLIC, AND THERE IS A CHARGE FOR THAT SERVICE IN MANY PLACES. THIS CHARGE IS NOT PAYABLE TO SMC, ONLY TO THE NOTARY PUBLIC FOR HIS/HER SERVICES.

This copy of the contract is strictly for review and not for signing. So please feel free to write all over it, make notes, and so on. Once we are all in agreement, and are ready to proceed forward, I will give you a clean copy of the contract to sign.

SAMPLE MANAGEMENT CO., Inc.
555 Fifty-fifth St.
Los Angeles, CA 90036

SAMPLE MANAGEMENT CO., INC.—PERSONAL MANAGEMENT CONTRACT

SIGNATURE INSTRUCTION MAP

Please follow this *Signature Instruction Map* when completing this contract. Please sign only the areas designated by this guide.

Page 5/Bottom

- Fill in date
- Young actor signs *Artist Signature*, parent(s) signs *Parent Signature*

Page 6/Bottom Only

- Please do not date this page
- Young actor signs *Artist Signature*, parent(s) signs *Parent Signature*
- Please do not fill in "To:" space at top of this page

Page 7

- This page requires the services of a notary public before any signatures are put to paper
- Parent(s) should sign *Parent Signature* in the presence of a notary public
- Notary public will fill in the other spaces

Page 8

- Please do not date this page
- Young actor signs *Artist Signature*, parent(s) signs *Parent Signature*

Page 9

- Please do not date this page
- Young actor signs *Artist Signature*
- Young actor should initial each of the lines titled *Artist's Initials*
- Parent should place his/her initials underneath the *Artist Signature* line

SAMPLE MANAGEMENT CO., Inc.
555 Fifty-fifth St.
Los Angeles, CA 90036

<u>SAMPLE MANAGEMENT CO., INC.—PERSONAL MANAGEMENT
CONTRACT</u>

<u>ARTIST'S/MANAGER'S AGREEMENT</u>

THIS AGREEMENT is made and entered into at Los Angeles County
by and between Mr. Joe Schmoe (hereinafter known as MANAGER) of
SAMPLE MANAGEMENT CO., Inc., and **New Client** (hereinafter
known as ARTIST), of **1234 N. Client Street, Los Angeles, California
11111** and **Mom and Dad New Client** (PARENT/LEGAL GUARDIAN,
hereinafter known as PARENT), of **1234 N. Client Street, Los Angeles,
California 11111.**

1. THIS AGREEMENT shall begin on date here and shall be for a
    period of 3 (three) years. Upon expiration of the stated term,
    this agreement shall remain in full force and effect without
    interruption or change unless and until either party notifies the
    other in writing by Certified Mail of *Intent to Terminate*. Such
    termination shall be effective immediately upon receipt. Nothing
    in any part of this agreement shall be interpreted to allow
    Artist or Parent to unilaterally terminate this agreement before
    the stated term has expired.

2. ARTIST AND PARENT EMPLOY MANAGER to act as Artist's
    sole and exclusive Personal Manager throughout the world with
    respect to all phases of the agreement in writing. Artist and
    Parent specifically agree that Manager is at all times an inde-
    pendent contractor, and that this agreement shall not constitute a
    joint venture or partnership between Manager and Artist and/or
    Parent. Manager is not a talent agent and is not expected to per-
    form any of the legal duties of a talent agent, including solicita-
    tion, procurement, and/or negotiation of employment for Artist.
    Manager may also represent other clients in addition to Artist.

3. AS COMPENSATION FOR SERVICES under this agreement, Manager shall be entitled to a commission of 10% (ten percent) of all gross monies or other considerations paid to Artist, exclusive of any per diem payments or reimbursements for travel or wardrobe, or employment remuneration or other receipts unrelated to the Entertainment Industry, but including payments for merchandising or any other promotional efforts, or bona fide offers of employment made during the term of this agreement, regardless of when Artist may receive such payments, even after the term of this agreement has expired.

4. ARTIST SHALL NOT RECEIVE PAYMENTS or remunerations directly. All payments to Artist under this agreement shall be paid to Artist through Manager's Talent Trust Account. Manager shall deduct commissions and any other monies due Manager and disperse balance to Artist's current address. Artist and Parent shall not at any time during this agreement, or after the term of this agreement has expired, engage in any action to divert receipt of payments or compensations due under the terms of this agreement from being transmitted to Manager and paid through Manager's Talent Trust Account. Such payments to Artist and Parents will be made within 7 (seven) days. Manager will include with such check a written summary specifying the sums received and their source, the deductions made, the purpose therefore, and the balance payable.

5. ARTIST REPRESENTS that he/she can freely make this agreement, and that he/she will make all reasonable efforts to set aside other commitments in order to meet any obligations under this agreement for interviews/auditions, classes/workshops, and engagements.

6. MANAGER REPRESENTS THAT he is prepared to represent Artist suitably in the Entertainment Industry. At such time as Manager feels unable to provide such representation for any reason, Manager will notify Artist promptly in writing. Such notification by Manager shall be grounds for avoiding this agreement,

except Manager shall be entitled to all commissions, as described in Section 3, for work performed or derived from commitments made during the term of this agreement before termination.

7. MANAGER WILL PROVIDE ARTIST with advice and counsel on all matters concerning Artist's career in the Entertainment Industry, being truthful at all times. Manager will make no binding engagement in Artist's behalf without Artist's consent.

8. ARTIST AND PARENT APPOINT MANAGER as Artist's lawful Attorney-in-Fact, to perform any and all services, execute any and all documents, and do any and all things necessary pursuant to this agreement. To reinforce this authority, Parent agrees, upon request, to execute before a Notary Public, a separate Power of Attorney for Manager. The authority granted by this section is coupled with an interest and shall be irrevocable during the term of this agreement. Nothing in this section shall be construed to allow Artist or Parent to revoke Manager's right to receive payments or endorse checks on behalf of Artist as provided in Section 4, even after the term of this agreement has expired.

9. THIS AGREEMENT CANNOT be changed in any way, except by the consent of both parties in writing, and shall be interpreted according to the laws of the State of California. Artist and Parent and Manager agree that any dispute or claim of whatever nature arising out of, in connection with, or in relation to the interpretation, performance, default, or breach of this agreement will be resolved through a two-step dispute resolution process administered by the Judicial Arbitration and Mediation Services, Inc. (hereafter called JAMS), involving first mediation before a retired judge from the JAMS panel of mediators or arbitrators followed, if necessary, by submission to final and binding arbitration conducted at a location within Los Angeles, California, as determined by the arbitrator before a retired judge from the JAMS panel of arbitrators administered by and in accordance with JAMS then-prevailing Rules of Practice and Procedure and not by a lawsuit or resort to court process except

as California law provides for judicial review of arbitration proceedings. Artist and Parent and Manager, by entering into this agreement, understand that they are giving up their right to have any such dispute or claim decided in a court of law before a jury and instead are accepting the use of arbitration. This arbitration agreement shall apply to any legal claim or civil action in connection with the obligations of or services rendered by Manager, its agents, or employees or the obligations of Artist and Parent including, but not limited to, funds or commissions due to Manager. The prevailing party in such arbitration and any action arising herefrom will recover reasonable attorney's fees and statutory costs. Any waiver by Manager, Artist, or Parent of any breach by Manager, Artist, or Parent of any provision of this agreement shall not be construed as a waiver of any subsequent breach by Manager, Artist, or Parent. In the event any portion of this agreement shall not extend to any other portion of this agreement, the remaining portions of this agreement shall remain in full force and effect.

10. REGARDLESS OF ANY ACTION Artist may take in the future pertaining to disaffirmance of this agreement, whether successful or not, such action will not cancel, void, or avoid Parent's obligation under this agreement, and Parent agrees to take no action which might influence Artist to breach, disaffirm, or terminate this agreement. Parent is liable for commissions due Manager under this agreement, regardless of any action taken by Artist, and it is specifically agreed that all services performed by Manager are equally beneficial to both Artist and Parent.

11. ARTIST AND PARENT acknowledge that Manager has, upon request, explained any and all provisions of this agreement, and that Artist and Parent have had ample opportunity, if so desired, to consult with and receive the advice of an Attorney-at-Law before signing this agreement. Parent does hereby acknowledge having read and understood this agreement, and does hereby agree and guarantee to comply or cause compliance with all of its provisions.

Date

Artist (Print)   New Client   **Signature** _____

Parent/Guardian (Print)   Mom New Client   **Signature** _____

Parent/Guardian (Print)   Dad New Client   **Signature** _____

Manager   Joe Schmoe   **Signature** _____

SAMPLE MANAGEMENT CO., Inc.
555 Fifty-fifth St.
Los Angeles, CA 90036

AUTHORIZATION TO SEND PAYMENTS TO ARTIST'S PERSONAL MANAGER

To:
Re: New Client

I hereby authorize Mr. Joe Schmoe, my Personal Manager, to accept delivery of any and all checks, drafts, and/or sums of money, or other forms of compensation, payment, or remuneration, for my services in the Entertainment Industry, which may from time to time become due and payable, and I hereby authorize and direct delivery of such checks, drafts, payments, or other forms of remuneration as follows:

> SAMPLE MANAGEMENT CO., Inc.
> Talent Trust
> 555 Fifty-fifth St.
> Los Angeles, CA 90036
> Attn: Mr. Joe Schmoe

Or to such other address as Mr. Schmoe may provide.

I agree that Mr. Schmoe is entitled to receive all monies or other considerations under the terms of our ARTIST'S/MANAGER'S AGREEMENT, and I will make no attempt at any time to prevent or otherwise interfere with your directing such payments through the ARTISTS MANAGEMENT NETWORK either during the term of our agreement, or with regard to such payments as may be commissionable to Mr. Joe Schmoe after such agreement has expired.

I also herby authorize you to supply Mr. Schmoe, upon his request, with copies, at his expense, of any accounting records pertinent to my income, as he may desire.

This authorization is coupled with an interest and may not be revoked at any time, except by written notice, signed by Mr. Joe Schmoe and myself, and delivered to you by "Certified Mail—Return Receipt Requested."

This authorization supersedes any prior authorization which you may have on file.

Date

Artist (Print)   New Client   **Signature** _____

Parent/Guardian (Print)   Mom and Dad New Client

                                        Signature _____

SAMPLE MANAGEMENT CO., Inc.
555 Fifty-fifth St.
Los Angeles, CA 90036

SPECIAL POWER OF ATTORNEY

BE IT HEREBY KNOWN THAT this Power of Attorney, as attested by the undersigned, **Mom and Dad New Client,** of **1234 N. Client Street, Los Angeles, California 11111,** does hereby authorize and empower Mr. Joe Schmoe to act on behalf of my/our child, **New Client (SS#000-00-0000)** as Personal Manager for my child's work in the Entertainment Industry, and to sign any and all documents relating to such work. I grant Mr. Joe Schmoe full power of decision and acceptance of contractual employment and/or compensation.

IN ACKNOWLEDGEMENT HEREOF, I have hereunto set my hand this **30th** day of **Month, 2XXX,** at **Los Angeles County.**
Parent/Guardian (Print)   Mom and Dad New Client
                                                    Signature _____

State of California
On   before me, personally appeared,_____,
personally known to me, or proved to me on the basis of satisfactory evidence, to be the person whose name is subscribed to the within instrument and acknowledged to me that he/she executed the same in his/her authorized capacity, and that by his/her signature on the person upon behalf of which the person acted, executed the instrument.

WITNESS my hand and official seal.

Notary Public _____

SAMPLE MANAGEMENT CO., Inc.
555 Fifty-fifth St.
Los Angeles, CA 90036

DIRECTIVE TO SCREEN ACTORS GUILD (SAG)

Date_____

Please accept this letter as your authorization to change/list my mailing address as follows:

> To: New Client
> c/o SAMPLE MANAGEMENT CO., Inc.
> 555 Fifty-fifth St.
> Los Angeles, CA 90036

Please send all communications for me to the above address, as well as all residual checks not otherwise commissionable to the agent.

THIS AUTHORIZATION WILL REMAIN IN EFFECT UNTIL REVOKED BY ME IN WRITING.

Thank you.

Artist	**New Client**	**Signature** _____
Parent/Guardian	**Mom and Dad New Client**	**Signature** _____
Current Address	_____	
City	_____	
State	_____	
ZIP	_____	
Home Phone	_____	
SS#	_____	

SAMPLE MANAGEMENT CO., Inc.
555 Fifty-fifth St.
Los Angeles, CA 90036

DIRECTIVE TO THE AMERICAN FEDERATION OF RADIO & TELEVISION ARTISTS

AFTRA
6922 Hollywood Blvd.
P.O. Box 4070
Hollywood, California 90078-4070   *Re: AUTHORIZATION—*
TALENT CHECKS

AFTRA
I HEREBY AUTHORIZE AND DIRECT YOU TO DELIVER ANY AND ALL CHECKS AND/OR SUMS OF MONEY WHICH MAY, FROM TIME TO TIME, BE OR BECOME PAYABLE TO ME INCLUDING BUT NOT LIMITED TO INITIAL COMPENSATION, RESIDUALS, ROYALTIES, RE-PLAY AND FOREIGN USE PAYMENTS, UNLESS LIMITED TO SERVICES CHECKED AND INITIALED BY ME BELOW, TO MY PERSONAL MANAGER:

> To: *New Client*
> SAMPLE MANAGEMENT CO., Inc.
> 555 Fifty-fifth St.
> Los Angeles, CA 90036
> Attn: Mr. Joe Schmoe

- THIS AUTHORIZATION SHALL REMAIN IN EFFECT UNTIL WRITTEN NOTICE OF THE REVOCATION THEREOF, EXE-CUTED AND ACKNOWLEDGED BY ME, SHALL BE RECEIVED BY YOU.
- THIS AUTHORIZATION SUPERSEDES ANY PRIOR DATED AUTHORIZATION THAT YOU MAY HAVE ON FILE REGARD-ING DELIVERY OF CHECKS AND/OR SUMS OF MONEY PAY-BLE TO ME.

Very Truly Yours,

Artist   New Client   Signature_____
Social Security Number 000-00-0000

THIS AUTHORIZATION IS LIMITED TO THE FOLLOWING: <u>ARTIST MUST INITIAL BELOW</u>

Network, Local, and Syndicated TV Programs
                         ARTIST'S INITIALS_____
Program Promos   ARTIST'S INITIALS_____
Radio and TV Commercials ARTIST'S INITIALS_____
Voice-Overs   ARTIST'S INITIALS_____
Phonograph Recordings   ARTIST'S INITIALS_____
Nonbroadcast, Industrials, Slide Film Records
                         ARTIST'S INITIALS_____

SPECIFIC AUTHORIZATION: THIS AUTHORIZATION SHALL APPLY TO THE FOLLOWING <u>SPECIFIC CHECKS ONLY AND NO OTHERS</u>:

GLOSSARY

Action: What a director or first assistant director yells to begin all of the main action in a scene.

AD: The assistant director. The first assistant director works closely with the director at all times. The second AD is usually in charge of the background or extra performers, including checking them in, preparing their wardrobes, and so on.

Ad Lib: A piece of dialogue or action that is done on the spur of the moment without a script or forethought.

AFI: The American Film Institute.

ADR: Additional dialogue replacement. This is a rerecording of the dialogue in a scene due to excess noise on the set or other technical issues. Sometimes this is called *looping*.

Affiliate: A local television station that carries a major network's programming, such as ABC, CBS, NBC, WB, or PAX.

AFTRA: The American Federation of Television and Radio Artists union.

Agent: A professional who pitches her or his clients for a particular project.

Agency: A large organization that has many agents.

ATA: The Association of Talent Agents.

Audition: A tryout for a particular role that can result in a callback for another audition.

Background: Term used to refer to background performers in a scene. Also the verbal cue given for the background actors to start walking before the main action takes place.

Back to One: A verbal cue given to background performers to return to the spot they started at in the scene.

Billing: The order of performers' names at the beginning or end of a show's credits.

Bio: A biography. Usually a short description of experience and personal facts.

Blocking: Planning the movement in the scene so the director, cinematographer, and actors know where to be at any given moment.

Blue Book: A publication detailing regulations regarding the employment of minors in the entertainment industry. Published by the Studio Teachers of the International Alliance of Theatrical Stage Employees Local 884.

Breakdown: A listing of available roles in various TV shows and films distributed to agents.

Bump: Term used to describe a situation in which a background performer is given a specific task to perform or one line to say.

Callback: A follow-up audition before being cast in a production.

Call Sheet: A daily listing of set numbers, times, and cast members needed for a particular scene or scenes.

Call Time: A specific time that an actor is expected to be on set to check in with the production.

Camera Left: Your right while on set.

Camera Right: Your left while on set.

Casting Director: The person directly responsible for hiring performers for a particular production under the supervision of the producer and the director.

Cattle Call: A general audition where hundreds of people try out for a part. Also called an *open call*.

Clapboard: A piece of wood or metal that contains information about a scene such as the scene number, the take number, and the director's name. Used on camera to both mark the start of the scene and to synchronize audio with the clapping sound.

Close-Up: A very tight shot, usually of a face or eyes.

Cold Reading: An unrehearsed reading of a script at an audition.

Composite: A single photograph made up of smaller individual photographs, usually showcasing different wardrobes and activities.

Coogan Law: Senate Bill 1162. Sets aside 15 percent of a child's earnings in a trust account.

Copy: The lines for a commercial. Also called a *script*.

Craft Services: The people responsible for the on-set catering.

Credits: A list of people involved in the production.

Cue: A verbal or nonverbal way for the director to give direction to actors and the crew.

Cut: A verbal cue to indicate that the actors and the cinematographer should stop their performance.

Dark: A period of time a production is on hiatus.

Day Player: An actor hired for a specific role for a short period of time.

Demo Tape: A cassette tape, compact disc, or videotape either used to obtain an agent or used by agents to secure work for the performer.

Dialect: A particular way of saying words based on the geographic origins of a character.

Director: The person who coordinates the filming of a production.

Dupe: A copy of a demo reel cassette or videotape.

Emancipated: A designation given by the state in which a minor is considered an adult and not bound by the work regulations for minors even if under the age of eighteen.

Extra: A performer used to provide atmosphere in a scene. Also called *background actor*.

Glossy: A shiny photographic finish of a headshot or composite.

Headshot: An eight-by-ten-inch photograph of an actor focusing mainly on the facial features.

Hiatus: A period of time that a production is closed down. Usually occurs during the winter for a few weeks and then over the summer.

Honey Wagon: A series of trailers used as dressing rooms.

Hot Set: A set that has been lit and dressed so that it is ready for filming. A nice way to say, "Do not touch."

IATSE: International Alliance of Theatrical Stage Employees union. Studio Teachers belong to Local 884.

IMTA: International Modeling and Talent Association.

Industrial: A production shot on videotape or film that is used internally by a company to train its employees.

In the Can: Slang term meaning that the production is filmed, edited, and ready for distribution.

Lithograph: A form of eight-by-ten photograph that is cheaper to reproduce than a glossy photo but does not have the same resolution.

Manager: A businessperson who advises your career and handles distribution of funds from your agent.

Mark: A piece of tape on the floor to tell the actor when to stop walking.

Moving On: A verbal cue to the production staff that a scene has been completed and they should get ready for the next one.

MOW: Movie of the week.

On a Bell: A verbal cue given to the production staff that signals filming is about to begin.

One Bell: A bell that is rung to designate that filming is about to commence.

Open Call: An audition that is open to anybody to attend. Sometimes called a *cattle call*.

PA: A production assistant.

Principals: The main actors in the scene, usually those listed in the opening credits.

Print: A verbal cue from the director that lets the crew know the take they just shot is good.

Proof Sheet: An eight-by-ten-inch photograph that contains little pictures of the entire roll of film shot. From this you usually pick two to three of the best ones to have enlarged and then pick out your final headshot.

Producer: The main coordinator of a production.

Prop: A small or large item that is physically handled in a scene.

PSA: Public service announcement.

Publicist: A professional representative who is in charge of coordinating interviews and appearances to increase an actor's visibility.

Résumé: A list of film, television, and theatre roles an actor has been in. Also lists information such as height, weight, and hobbies.

Roach Wagon: An unflattering term used for a small RV-type vehicle that caters hot and cold drinks and other food items.

Rolling: A verbal cue given to let the production crew know that film is being passed through the camera.

Script: A written document that contains the dialogue, location, and various directions of a scene. Also called *copy*.

Slate: A verbal cue given by the director to use the clapboard to mark the beginning or end of a scene.

Speed: A verbal cue given to let the director know that the film and audio have both synchronized and are rolling at full speed.

Stage Right: Your right when on set.

Stage Left: Your left when on set.

SAG: Screen Actors Guild, a labor union for film actors.

SB 1162: Senate Bill 1162. Puts aside 15 percent of a child performer's earnings into a court-approved trust account. Also called the *Coogan Law*.

Scale: A minimum pay amount for a particular role.

Scale Plus 10: The minimum pay amount for a particular role plus 10 percent to cover the agency commission.

SEG: Screen Extras Guild.

Set: The physical environment the actors are placed into to film a scene.

Sides: An excerpt of a script used for auditioning purposes.

Sight and Sound: The maximum distance a parent should be from his or her child while on the set.

Stand-In: A person who is used to help light the scene so that the main actor does not have to do it.

Sticks: A large version of a clapboard without the writing on it, used to synchronize sound.

Studio Teacher: A teacher who has both elementary and secondary teaching credentials and has passed the certification to teach on the set.

Taft-Hartley: Legislation that allows an actor to appear in a union production before he joins the union.

Take: A specific version of a scene.

Trades: Publications such as *The Hollywood Reporter, Variety,* and *Back Stage West.*

Trailer: A short film about an upcoming movie or television show shown before the feature presentation.

Two Bells: An audio cue on the set that is used to let everybody know that a specific take is over.

Union: An organization that works to improve and maintain working conditions and standards for its members.

Upgrade: An increase in visibility and pay scale from background to day player or to featured. Sometimes called a *bump.*

Work Permit: A permit issued to a young performer for the period of six months allowing her to work if she is under sixteen.

Wrap: The end of a particular production after all scenes are shot.